PHOTOGRAPHY YEAR

Home Repair and Improvement
The Time-Life Library of Boating
Human Behavior
The Art of Sewing
The Old West
The Emergence of Man
The American Wilderness
The Time-Life Encyclopedia of Gardening
Life Library of Photography
This Fabulous Century
Foods of the World
Time-Life Library of America
Time-Life Library of Art
Great Ages of Man
Life Science Library
The Life History of the United States
Time Reading Program
Life Nature Library
Life World Library
Family Library:
   How Things Work in Your Home
   The Time-Life Book of the Family Car
   The Time-Life Family Legal Guide
   The Time-Life Book of Family Finance

PHOTOGRAPHY YEAR
1976 EDITION
BY THE EDITORS OF TIME-LIFE BOOKS

TIME LIFE BOOKS, NEW YORK

© 1976 Time Inc. All rights reserved.
First printing. Published simultaneously in Canada.
Library of Congress catalogue card number 75-37189.

ON THE COVER: A study of motion in color and a closeup of a new pocket-camera flash unit exemplify the visual excitement and technological innovations that were part of the past year in photography. The blurred rodeo cowboy and his bucking horse are from a 1975 book on America by the Austrian-born photographer Ernst Haas. General Electric's 1975 improved flash attachment for model 110 cameras places each bulb far enough above the lens to minimize the glare that, in other designs, often reflects in a subject's eyes.

Contents

Trends	9
The Major Shows	41
Discoveries	81
Assignment	119
The New Technology	137
The Annual Awards	165
The Year's Books	185
Roundup	215

Bibliography and Acknowledgments	239
Picture Credits	240
Index	241

TIME-LIFE BOOKS

FOUNDER: Henry R. Luce 1898-1967

Editor-in-Chief: Hedley Donovan
Chairman of the Board: Andrew Heiskell
President: James R. Shepley

Vice Chairman: Roy E. Larsen

MANAGING EDITOR: Jerry Korn
Assistant Managing Editors: Ezra Bowen, David Maness, Martin Mann, A. B. C. Whipple
Planning Director: Oliver E. Allen
Art Director: Sheldon Cotler
Chief of Research: Beatrice T. Dobie
Director of Photography: Melvin L. Scott
Senior Text Editors: Diana Hirsh, William Frankel
Assistant Planning Director: Carlotta Kerwin
Assistant Art Director: Arnold C. Holeywell
Assistant Chief of Research: Myra Mangan

PUBLISHER: Joan D. Manley
General Manager: John D. McSweeney
Business Manager: John Steven Maxwell
Sales Director: Carl G. Jaeger
Promotion Director: Paul R. Stewart
Public Relations Director: Nicholas Benton

EDITORIAL STAFF FOR PHOTOGRAPHY YEAR

EDITOR: Edward Brash
Picture Editor: Patricia Hunt
Designer: Thomas S. Huestis
Text Editor: John Man
Staff Writers: Don Earnest, James A. Randall
Researchers: Fran Ahders, Karen M. Bates, Thomas D. Dickey, Gretchen Wessels
Art Assistant: Patricia Byrne

Editorial Production
Production Editor: Douglas B. Graham
Assistant Production Editors: Gennaro C. Esposito, Feliciano Madrid
Quality Director: Robert L. Young
Assistant Quality Director: James J. Cox
Associate: Serafino J. Cambareri
Copy Staff: Eleanore W. Karsten (chief), Mary Ellen Slate, Florence Keith, Pearl Sverdlin
Picture Department: Dolores A. Littles, Martin Baldessari
Traffic: Carmen McLellan

Consultant for The New Technology:
Melvin J. Ingber

Valuable assistance was given by the following departments and individuals of Time Inc.: Editorial Production, Norman Airey; Library, Benjamin Lightman; Picture Collection, Doris O'Neil; TIME-LIFE Photo Lab, George Karas, Herbert Orth, Albert Schneider; John Durniak and Arnold H. Drapkin, TIME magazine; TIME-LIFE News Service, Murray J. Gart; Correspondents Margot Hapgood (London), Maria Vincenza Aloisi and Josephine du Brusle (Paris), Elisabeth Kraemer (Bonn), Ann Natanson (Rome), Eva Stichova (Prague), Anne Callahan (Washington, D.C.), Bernard Diederich (Mexico City), Frank Iwama (Tokyo), Mary Johnson (Stockholm), Lance Keyworth (Helsinki), Robert Kroon (Geneva), Traudl Lessing (Vienna), Sue Masterman (Rijswijk, Netherlands), John Shaw and Felix Rosenthal (Moscow), Barry Waters (Belgrade).

Introduction

It was the year of the personal statement in photography. In the United States, talented cadres of newspaper photographers were turning away from stereotypes of action and violence for quieter, more contemplative pictures that focused on the individual. Jerry Gay of *The Seattle Times,* for example, captured the stunning finality of a ruinous fire by photographing not the flames but the exhausted and dejected firemen who could not extinguish the blaze. He was among those praised by one critic for being "not walking cameras but thinking cameramen."

In London, Paris and New York, other innovators were revitalizing fashion photography. In their hands, fashion pictures rose above the familiar staid cliché to become visualizations of the photographers' private fantasies and dreams. These breezy, funny and often sexy pictures not only created a new genre—they also helped to sell clothes.

This trend toward a more personal and subjective approach was evident all through the world of photography. In Japan, the long-standing tradition of exquisite restraint was blatantly intruded upon by two highly idiosyncratic photojournalists. In one of the year's best books, *A Fine Day,* magazine photographer Kishin Shinoyama created a unique counterpoint of close-ups and long shots in color, while documentarian Shin Yanagisawa's candid eye plucked from a working-class festival the awkward struggle between modernity and tradition that Yanagisawa sees as part of his own life. In Czechoslovakia, despite official encouragement of socially oriented realism in the arts, a former steelworker turned photographer evoked the sensual beauty of turn-of-the-century European bohemia in his studies of nudes.

Even in the realm of pure technology, the most significant advances were in the direction of enabling the photographer to make notable personal statements. The Swiss firm of Ciba-Geigy introduced a home color process that drastically reduced the fuss required to produce rich, fade-resistant color prints, encouraging the home processor to convert his favorite slides into hang-on-the-wall prints. Most unique and striking of all, inexpensive equipment for the exacting art of holography now makes it possible for the serious home technician to make and project three-dimensional images that appear to be real sculptures hanging in air.

The Editors

… Trends/1

Trends / 1

New Eye for What's News	12
Radical Turn of Fashion	24

Turn of Fashion/ SARAH MOON: *Accessories and Make-up,* 1973

Trends

A New Eye For What's News

Photojournalists are now venturing beyond straight reportage to put sensitive and perceptive photograghs on the nation's front pages

In 1975, Pulitzer prizes went to two young photographers who are in the forefront of a bold new movement in daily newspaper photojournalism in the United States. The pictures that won acclaim for *The Seattle Times'* Jerry Gay and the *Chicago Tribune*'s Ovie Carter *(pages 183-184)* are light-years away from action shots like the exploding zeppelin *Hindenburg (page 228)* that have been stereotypes of front-page photography. The new wave is dramatic yet unsensational, well-composed but informative; quite suddenly newspaper photography has become creative photojournalism, indistinguishable from the best of the photography magazines.

This transformation of daily illustrations began in the Midwest and has flowered there. Its leader, Rich Clarkson, is a gifted photojournalist who has been director of photography of the *Topeka Capital-Journal* for 15 years. Although only 43, Clarkson has become something of a legend. In 1960 he instituted an internship program at the Topeka papers. Successful applicants —sometimes newcomers, sometimes pros looking for a refresher course —received valuable on-the-job training as they covered a regular beat for a three-month period, and absorbed the Clarkson doctrine. By the mid-1970s Clarkson's influence had spread to dailies—and weeklies—throughout the country. He insists that his staff photographers and interns aim for pictures that will cause the reader to think, or feel, deeply about human consequences rather than focus on an instant of concentrated action.

To get such pictures, the new photojournalists employ several techniques. Some of them look offstage for subjects. Anestis Diakopoulos of the *Providence Journal-Bulletin* in Rhode Island used a routine assignment—to cover a city council meeting—to produce the photograph at right, which illustrates not the debate itself but a bored night watchman waiting grumpily for its ending so that he can lock up and go home. Other photographers imaginatively exploit the technical capacities of cameras and lenses to drive home a point with symbolism. To capture the unusual image on page 16, Ovie Carter shot through a telephoto lens, and succeeded in evoking the doleful aura of deceased Black Muslim leader Elijah Muhammad, who from a gigantic poster seems to look down on his successor. In another example *(page 23)* James Mayo used a wide-angle lens, from a kneeling position, to turn an emblazoned Ku Klux Klanswoman into a towering, even menacing, figure.

Such arresting photographs find a receptive audience, helping to make newspapers visually provocative as well as informative. One man who is devoted to photographic quality is Brian Lanker, an ex-Clarkson photographer, who is now the director of photography of the *Eugene Register-Guard*. Lanker, whose own novel photograph appears overleaf, suggests that newspapers all over the United States may soon be staffed by men and women who will "not be walking cameras, but thinking cameramen."

ANESTIS DIAKOPOULOS, *The Providence Sunday Journal*, Rhode Island

A dour, bored night watchman waits in a deserted lobby for the city council of Central Falls, Rhode Island to conclude a late-night debate. Such telling, off-stage studies are a major element in the new wave of newspaper photojournalism in the United States.

Trends/**New Eye for What's News**

Two young nostalgia buffs show off their Bonnie and Clyde apparel, the turn-of-the-century hotel they have renovated and a mint-condition 1948 Hudson sedan parked at curbside.

BRIAN LANKER, *Eugene Register-Guard*, Oregon

The joyous downfall of a beer-drinking reveler, who never did make it to the track, captured the attention of photographer Schuhmann on Kentucky Derby day—a time when newsmen have traditionally focused on julep-sipping gentlemen and parading thoroughbreds.

PAUL SCHUHMANN, *The Courier-Journal & Times*, Louisville, Kentucky

Trends/**New Eye for What's News**

OVIE CARTER, *Chicago Tribune*, Illinois

◄ *Impassive eyes on a giant poster of the late Black Muslim leader Elijah Muhammad —brought dramatically close by a telephoto lens— loom over the Nation of Islam's newly selected spiritual head, Wallace Muhammad, as he is triumphantly hoisted onto the shoulders of the sect's elite guards and officers.*

Chin in hand, a bemused and defeated labor lobbyist grimaces as Kansas state senators swing toward approval of an antilabor bill. This insight into the back-room struggles of state politics came after the photographer had spent two months following the protagonists.

BERN KETCHUM, *The Topeka Daily Capital*, Kansas

Apparently unruffled by his fall from power to the status of a refugee, former premier and strong man of South Vietnam Nguyen Cao Ky relaxes in the unfurnished living room of the suburban Washington house rented for him and the 12 other members of his household.

CHARLES DEL VECCHIO, *The Washington Post*, District of Columbia

Trends/**New Eye for What's News**

MICHAEL LLOYD, *The Sunday Oregonian*, Portland, Oregon

The stunned and despairing face of a dory manufacturer dominates this photo taken on the morning a fire destroyed his 21-year-old business. The still-smoldering boatyard and the one surviving dory, at left, stand as mute testimony to the fire victim's loss.

Trends/**New Eye for What's News**

A 270-pound professional wrestler called the Mongolian Stomper contorts himself into a picture of agony—an instant captured by the photographer to convey the aura of stagey mayhem that is the epitome of the sport.

The damp resignation of a ferris-wheel operator ▶ and the wraithlike face of a ticket seller peering from beneath the lights of her cage create this perceptive look at a county fair on a rainy night.

TOM HAYS, *The Louisville Times*, Kentucky

JERRY GAY, *The Seattle Times*, Washington

Trends/**New Eye for What's News**

LINDA WHEELER, *The Washington Post*, District of Columbia

This portly, benign Washington, D.C. businessman posed for a homey portrait in his living room to accompany an interview on his commercial success. He is the leader of the city's pornography industry—"Sultan of an X-Rated Empire," the story's headline called him.

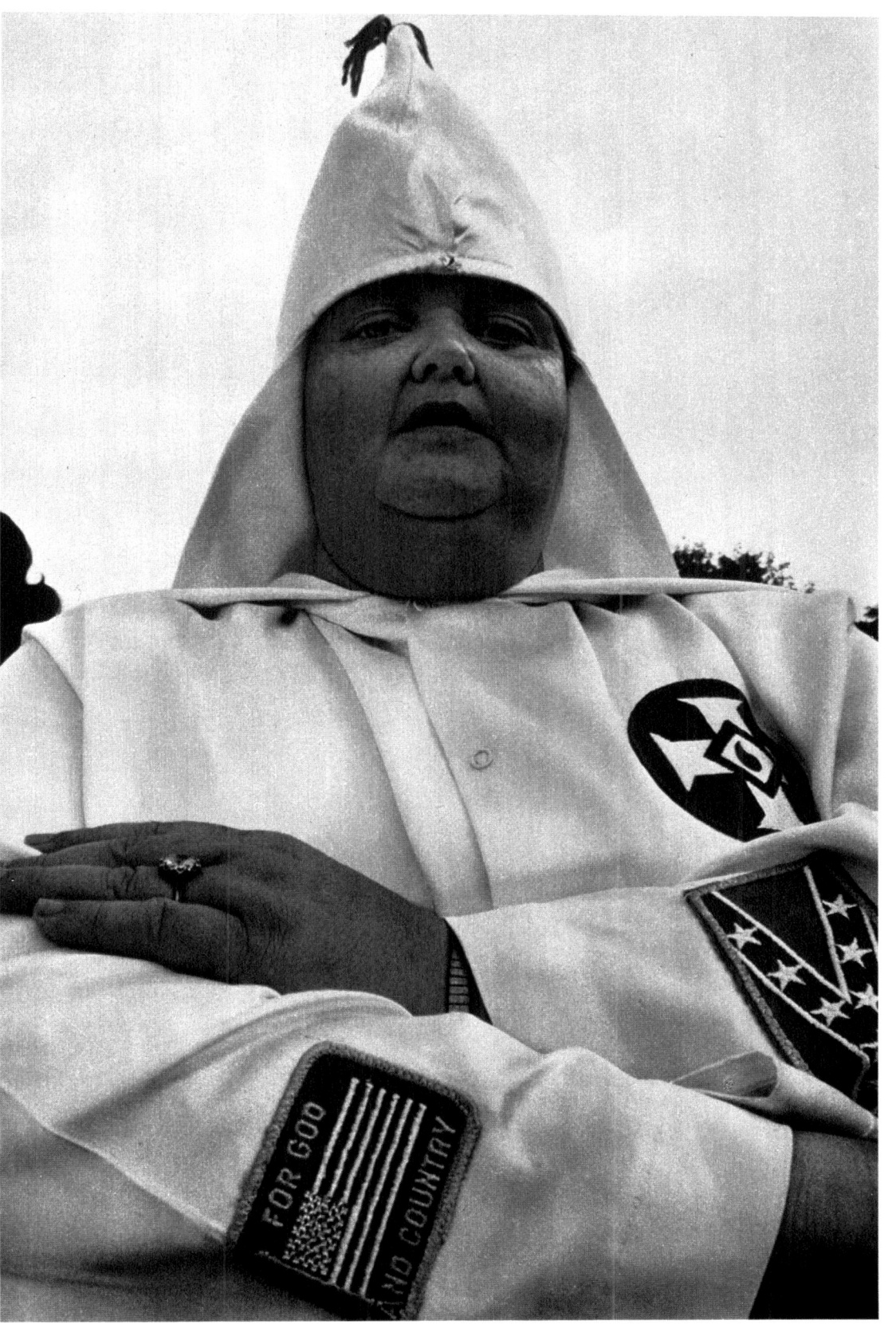

The overwhelming figure of a Klanswoman fills the frame of a photograph taken at a Ku Klux Klan rally in rural Indiana. The photographer exaggerated her dimensions by shooting from below with a wide-angle lens.

JAMES MAYO, *Chicago Tribune*, Illinois

Trends

A Radical Turn of Fashion

Photographs that combine fantasy, humor, narrative and sex are introducing an artful twist to the tough business of selling new clothes

A fresh wind is blowing through the staid salons of fashion photography, and riding upon it is a new pictorial approach that has unexpectedly turned fashion magazines into exciting showcases for photography. The daringly novel pictures are full of odd colors, fantastic images, ironic humor and offbeat sex. In fact, the pages of the May 1975 issue of *Vogue* magazine—where the new trend was dramatically introduced to American fashion readers—looked more like sophisticated movie stills or excerpts from interpretive news features than the photographic versions of dress-shop windows usually seen in fashion publications.

Two long photo essays highlighted the issue and startled readers. One was by the adroit and inventive Deborah Turbeville *(page 27)*, a 38-year-old former fashion editor who had become a career photographer only three years earlier. Her 10-page essay showed the latest styles in beach wear in a startling and bizarre setting, the deserted shower room of a public bathhouse in New York City. The other series of pictures, provocatively entitled *The Story of Ohhh . . .*, was by a German-born, Paris-based fashion veteran: Helmut Newton *(page 32)*. His essay, 14 pages in all, on summer clothes and perfumes depicted a series of bold encounters between men and women, with decidedly sexy overtones.

Together, Turbeville's innovations and Newton's provocations provided a long-awaited release for fashion photographers, who have languished in a stilted, tradition-minded world very much of their own making. When fashion photography first emerged as a genre in the 1910s and early 1920s, the pictures showed great society ladies draped in the latest styles and posed like wax statues in elaborate studio mockups of palatial salons and boudoirs. Ever since, photographers have been trying to pump more life into their art, but until now none had truly succeeded. By the late 1920s, elaborate settings had been replaced by plain backdrops, and some photographers began to shoot in real palaces and grand hotels. But the settings were basically still dead, and the models were as static and statuesque as ever.

In the mid-1930s, Martin Munkacsi, a Hungarian photojournalist turned fashion photographer, took his models out onto beaches and fields where they ran, jumped, skipped and laughed. Munkacsi's ebullient pictures temporarily transformed the art, and the next two decades saw the glorification of the outdoor girl in the more realistic settings of campus, beach or suburban picnic. But this concept, too, became an increasingly static cliché, as fashion editors and clothing manufacturers insisted that the pictures in final layouts stick to their primary job of showing off clothes, with all important hems and seams clearly visible.

Even the brilliant and perceptive Richard Avedon failed to force a permanent change—although in the early 1960s he made a gallant try by introducing the picture story to fashion essays. He patterned one 10-page sequence on a well-publicized affair between two movie stars. But despite Avedon's innovations, fashion models usually remained as two dimensional as cardboard cutouts.

The new concept began to take shape in Europe during the late 1960s, when fashion-magazine editors subtly encouraged—and then gave space to —an intriguing sort of photograph that showed action, real action. And they used models that looked more like hippies or tomboys than great ladies or girls next door. Although at first the movement was more evolutionary than revolutionary, it made a recognizable change in the appearance of several major European fashion magazines, most notably *Elle* and *Marie Claire* in France, *Nova* in England, and both the British and French editions of *Vogue*. The girls on these pages frowned, fell in love, went to parties, played the fool, or set off on incredible journeys to improbable places. When they were not actually on the go, they projected a mood of suspense and uncertainty suggesting that something had recently happened or was about to happen.

As soon as American editors perceived the vitality of this trend, and clothes makers saw it as a way to attract the eye to their product, the pages of United States fashion magazines took a quick and refreshing turn. The approach in American publications is basically narrative. The story line may be either explicit or implicit, and the pictures are usually fanciful. "I photograph my fantasies," says Newton. His fantasies are frankly erotic and the resulting images are often highly suggestive. For instance, he will enliven a nail-polish illustration by having a lady's richly bejeweled, pale hand clutch the firm, strong hand of a dark-skinned man *(page 32)*.

A different approach is used by Sarah Moon *(page 36)*, a young Parisian ex-model who has become one of Europe's most popular fashion photographers. Moon's photographs have a soft, dreamlike beauty. In one series, she records the adventures of a Chaplinesque model and waiflike children. In another, a bird-headed creature in a business suit accompanies a model on a fantastic train journey.

Satire is another important element in the new fashion photography. Many of the stories are tongue-in-cheek parodies of earlier photographic styles. Deborah Turbeville, for example, mocks the elegantly posturing ladies of former years when she shows two statuesque models in classic poses—and has a third puckishly kick up her heels *(page 30)*. Newton presents one sullen and perhaps tipsy lady, dressed to the nines, blowing cigarette smoke into another's face *(page 35)*.

To attain such effects, the photographers have adopted the tools and techniques of the photojournalist. They use 35mm cameras and have a marked preference for natural lighting. But in orchestrating their fantasies, they are

Trends/Turn of Fashion

more like theatrical directors. "Once I set up an idea, it's like a play," Deborah Turbeville notes. "You have a whole production company that can work for you: stylist; someone does hair; someone does makeup. It's a lot of people, a lot of collaboration. It turns you on."

These photographers are also like directors in the way they select casts for their stories. Instead of choosing models because they have beautiful and memorable faces or have figures suited to the fashion concept, the new image-makers search for a more elusive quality. In her interviews with models, Sarah Moon explains, "I am looking for a personality—not a face."

Equal care goes into the selection of locations. Describing her choice of the deserted public bathhouse as the setting for showing off the latest in swimwear *(page 28)*, Deborah Turbeville says, "It looked real and yet it's one step removed from reality for me. When you put five girls in a room like that —dressed like that—it becomes something beyond reality."

Once she has defined the space she is going to shoot in, Turbeville eases her models into casual poses. "Within my perimeters, I let them move freely, like interpretive dance," she says. Other photographers freeze motion. In one shot, Newton records two frolicking models tumbling into a swimming pool with the stop-action efficiency of a sports photographer *(page 34)*.

Some observers feel that the new fashion photographers are more interested in novel situations and settings than in their real job of selling clothes. Deborah Turbeville says no. To her, novelty and selling clothes go hand in hand: "Quite frankly, when I made those shower-room pictures, I wasn't considering the woman who was going to think of how the clothes would look on her. What I was trying to do was make an interesting picture. But when you make a photograph interesting, you are getting two things at once. You are showing clothes well, but you are also making magazine readers stop and spend more time than they ordinarily would on a fashion photograph. So, in the end, they are more likely to remember the clothes when they are buying." Even more likely, the new fashion photographs will be remembered long after the clothes they depict have gone out of style.

An Air of Mystery

"I love mystery—mystery stories and mystery films," says Deborah Turbeville, one of the two leaders of the dramatic turn in fashion photography. Reflecting this, her pictures often seem like illustrations for a detective story. Her settings are anonymous, like the hotel hallway at right; her models have a brooding, isolated quality. Her muted tones —mushroom whites and autumnal beiges, browns and oranges—enhance the feeling of remoteness. In addition the enigmas generated by this former fashion editor do exactly what all good fashion photographs are meant to do: pull the eye toward the creations of the world's top couturiers.

Deborah Turbeville by Duane Michals

Fresh-faced models, wearing Karl Lagerfeld's ready-to-wear garments, muse in a bare Paris hotel corridor.

An array of (from left) swim suits by Jean-Louis Scherrer, Stephen Burrows and Courrèges and a beach wrap by Ungaro create an unlikely grouping in a public bathhouse.

Trends/**Turn of Fashion**

A model sits marooned in a Bill Blass terry cloth jacket.

A casual Geoffrey Beene suit goes shopping at a chic salon.

Trends/**Turn of Fashion**

Evening dresses by Scott Barrie and Yves Saint Laurent bracket an elevated pair of gold slippers by Saint Laurent.

Sales ladies in basic black look with mild astonishment at a customer in a fully cut peasant blouse by Yves Saint Laurent.

In her all-white bedroom, English couturier Jean Muir (left) admires models draped in her suede dresses.

Trends/**Turn of Fashion**

Tough Chic

With their clashing hues and startling concepts, the brilliant, clear color of Helmut Newton's photographs comes dangerously close to being gaudy. But his harsh tones are eminently suited to the contemporary settings that he prefers. And they accentuate the passions and antics of his brash and aggressive models who suddenly intensify the meaning of a handclasp or get into slightly boozy contretemps.

At the same time, Newton uses play-offs on conventional impressions and techniques to contrast with his fresh images. For example, using long exposure and electronic flash, he made the hotel behind a running model *(opposite)* into a backdrop as dazzling as the diamond horseshoe of an opera house.

Self-portrait by Helmut Newton

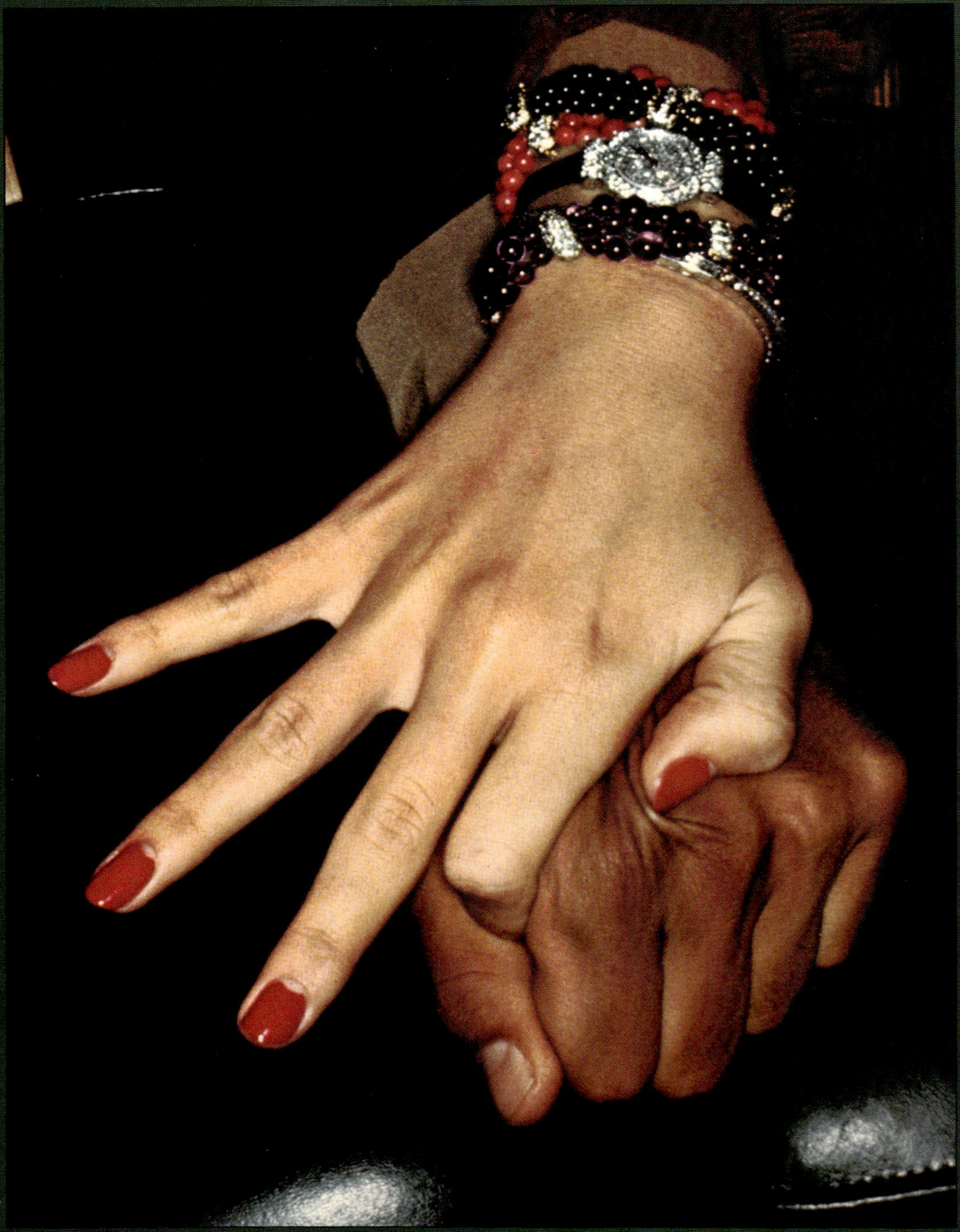

Fingers adorned with Elizabeth Arden's new nail polish transmit an intense message.

A young woman flees a Key Biscayne hotel wearing a see-through evening gown by Scott Barrie.

Riviera visitors in halters and skirts by Emmanuelle Khanh and Missoni dunk an escort at Eden Roc, Cap d'Antibes.

A classic—and somewhat surly—encounter occurs between cocktail-hour competitors in the same crocheted top by Loris Azzaro.

Trends/**Turn of Fashion**

Moon Glow

"I see out of focus naturally," says French photographer Sarah Moon, who is, in point of medical fact, myopic. She goes to great lengths to recreate in photographs her natural vision—by using filters, gauze, and even petroleum jelly smeared on her lens to soften her images.

Until 1967, Moon worked as a fashion model under her real name, Marielle Hadengue. "I posed for catalogues, I was never a star," she admits. But her fortunes changed when she switched careers. Now a recognized star, Moon strives for a romantic effect. Often she shoots models close up, but a faraway look clouds their eyes. Other times, she puts them in a nostalgic set. But there is always something melancholy about them, suggesting bittersweet adventures.

Sarah Moon by David Bailey

Their faces muted by the misty quality of the photograph, models in nunlike costume wear very secular cosmetics by Estée Lauder

and Lancaster.

Train windows frame a trendy young mother in a Sheridan Barnett suit standing with her brood at the station in Brighton, England.

A tousled adventuress in Janet Reger lingerie awaits a rendezvous.

An elegant passenger in a handpainted crepe suit by Karl Lagerfeld holds the hand of a mysterious companion.

Trends/**Turn of Fashion**

A young girl in a Cacharel dress floats down the staircase of an Egyptian hotel.

Dark-eyed beauties in Biba cosmetics evoke images from silent films.

The Major Shows / 2

The Major Shows / 2

Russia's Wartime Anguish	44
Living Color	56
Edward Weston	64

Living Color/ WILLIAM EGGLESTON: *Summer Afternoon Light in Greenwood, Mississippi,* 1974

The Major Shows

A Cry of Anguish from Wartime Russia

An exhibit in Prague closes a major gap in the photographic history of World War II

When the exhibition entitled "Soviet War Photo-Reportage 1941-1945" was announced in Prague, few Czech photography connoisseurs were prepared to witness a major event in photojournalism. The House of Soviet Science and Culture, where the show was to be held, has not been known for memorable photography; it has generally been a showcase for propagandish presentations of Soviet progress: streamlined power plants, friendly cosmonauts and smiling women tractor drivers. Few Czechs bother to go.

But this show was dramatically different, and it lured large numbers of frankly admiring Czechs to the hall—to see the finest collection of war photographs ever to appear in Eastern Europe. Despite the ferocity and extent of the fight on the Eastern Front—which took 20 million Russian lives—no such collection of Soviet war pictures had previously been known to exist. Indeed, pictures from the Eastern Front had been so rare that students of photography of the era might have assumed that there was little or no interest in the documentary approach among Russians.

In fact nothing could have been further from the truth. A strong realistic-photography tradition exists in the U.S.S.R., born in the '20s and nurtured by Lenin, who seized on the idea of using photography as a means of informing and inspiring a largely illiterate Russian people. From this concept came a generation of highly motivated and sophisticated photographers. And when Russia entered the war, men and women from this pool of skilled and sensitive artists went out to document it. But their work had been lost, or misplaced. Few of the pictures at the show in Prague had been viewed outside Russia, and even there, most had appeared only fleetingly during the short lives of wartime periodicals. Some had never been published at all.

A Czech couple rediscovered for Russia this dramatic chapter in their own photographic history. Daniela Mrázková, editor of the highly regarded Czech magazine *Fotografie,* and her husband, Vladimír Remeš, a correspondent for the same magazine, had long suspected that a trove of powerful Russian war pictures must exist, and they were determined to find it and put it on display. Learning that official Soviet archives were not able to produce exhibition-quality prints, and in any case did not have a full representation of the kind of images they wanted, Mrázková and Remeš got in touch with the photographers themselves—or their survivors. Carefully, painstakingly, the couple collected prints from personal files.

After three years and several trips to Russia, they completed their selection from the pictures of 20 men and one woman for the show. Only one of the photographers, Dmitri Baltermants, had already established an international reputation as a wartime photographer, but all had come from the same vital tradition. In the crucible of war, they trained their lenses on real individuals and captured images deserving of worldwide attention.

An agonizingly young political officer in the Red Army, his head swathed in bloody bandages, seems to be crying out in pain—but the photographer's records indicate that he was shouting orders. Although not trained to command men in the field, political officers often had to lead troops against the war machine.

IVAN SAGIN: *Political Officer Giving Combat Orders,* 1942

The Major Shows/**Russia's Wartime Anguish**

In a classic scene of winter warfare, a column of Soviet troops advances across a snow-covered field near Leningrad. A special eye for this kind of drama distinguishes much of the work of photographer Garanin who, besides being a photojournalist, has done a number of studies of theatrical productions.

ANATOLI GARANIN: *Leningrad Front,* 1942

*Rising out of the smoke of battle, marines of the
Black Sea Fleet counterattack near Tuapse,
a Caucasian port at which the German advance
toward Soviet oil fields was turned back.
The feeling of frozen motion, so like a movie still,
reflects Uzian's early training as a film maker.*

ALEXANDR UZIAN: *Black Sea Fleet*, 1942

The Major Shows/**Russia's Wartime Anguish**

In a log shelter far behind enemy lines, a weary night nurse reads by the light of a makeshift oil lamp. Behind her, wounded Russian civilian fighters sleep. The photographer, Mikhail Trakhman, made frequent trips into German-encircled pockets of resistance. In order to protect the identities of the underground fighters whom he had photographed, Trakhman carried a grenade in his film bag, ready to destroy his exposed rolls if captured.

MIKHAIL TRAKHMAN: *Field Hospital,* 1941

During the 900-day siege of Leningrad, a grief-stricken mother leaves the swaddled body of her infant in a cemetery. The child is one of nearly a million people who perished—primarily from cold and starvation—while the city was blockaded by the Germans.

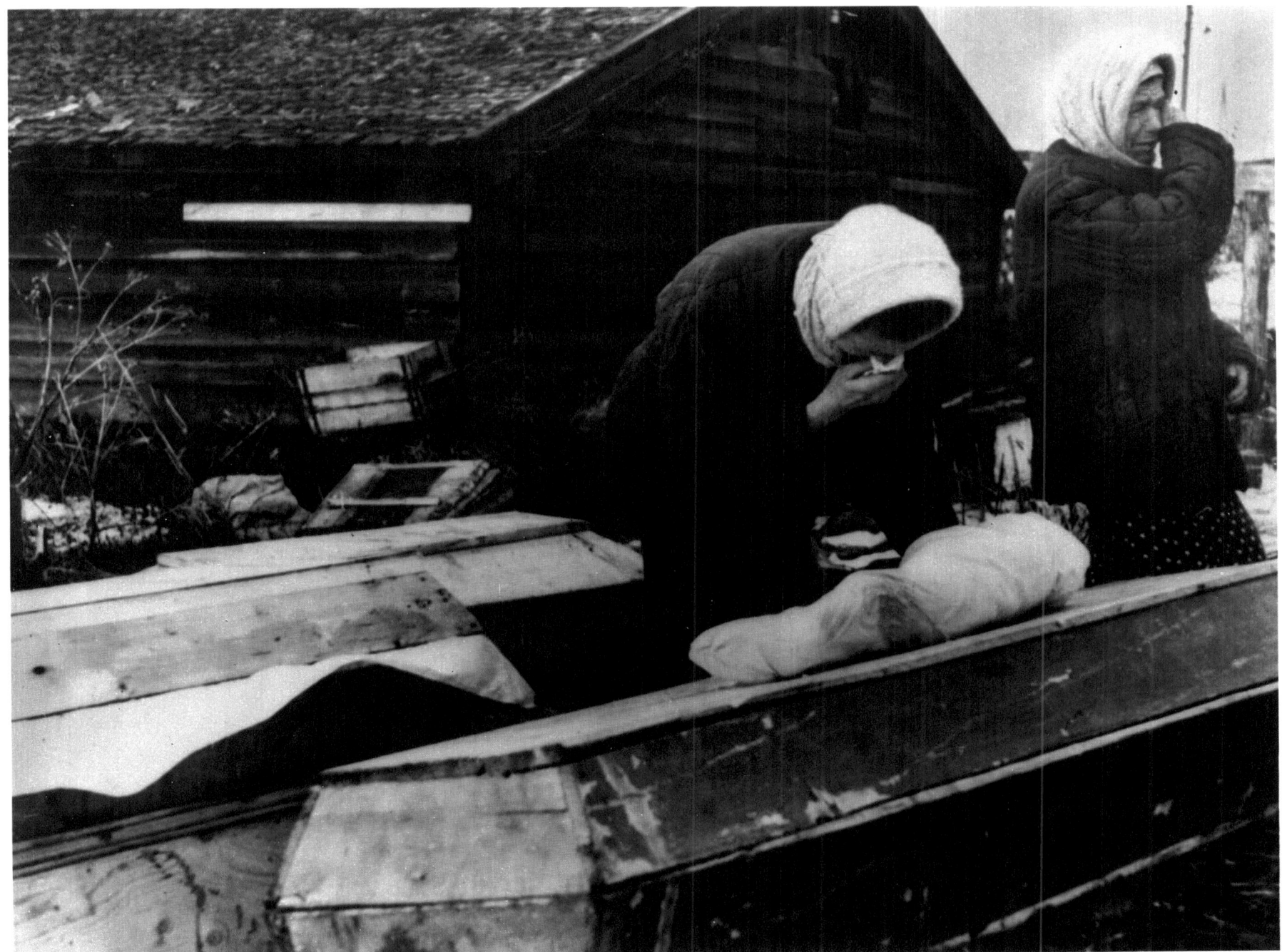

BORIS KUDOYAROV: *Volkovo Cemetery,* 1942

The Major Shows/**Russia's Wartime Anguish**

GALINA SANKOVA: *On Russian Soil,* 1941

This grim study of frozen, snow-covered German corpses—the face and upper body of one soldier and the hobnail boots of another—came from the camera of one of five Soviet women who covered the war. The picture was taken on the outskirts of Moscow where the bitter Russian winter halted Hitler's advance in 1941.

A lone Soviet soldier trudges past a mass grave filled with comrades and marked by a makeshift fence made of bedsteads. During the last savage weeks of the Battle of Stalingrad, more than 46,000 Russian soldiers were killed. After the war, most of these Russian fighters were reburied in regular cemeteries.

GEORGI ZELMA: *Mass Grave of Soviet Soldiers in Stalingrad,* 1943

The Major Shows/**Russia's Wartime Anguish**

A massive flotsam of Russian tanks and other materiel lies along Berlin's Moltke Bridge and the near bank of the River Spree. The bridge, inexplicably left intact by German engineers, opened the city's heart to Russian troops, and was bitterly contested by the defenders. Now, in the battle's aftermath, idle soldiers lounge against a bombed-out tank, and stray dogs wander amid the rubble.

VIKTOR GREBNEV: *The Route to the Reichstag,* 1945

The Major Shows/**Russia's Wartime Anguish**

Inside a ruined Berlin building, victorious Soviet soldiers relax around a piano, miraculously undamaged and topped with a vase of flowers. According to the photographer, the soldiers were playing the music of Tchaikovsky when this picture was taken.

A Russian soldier raises the Red Flag over the Reichstag shortly after Soviet troops had cleared the building of 5,000 German holdouts in two days of room-to-room combat.

DMITRI BALTERMANTS: *Tchaikovsky,* 1945

YEVGENI KHALDEY: Victory, 1945

The Major Shows

The Commonplace in Living Color

With hard-edged hues and oversized prints, William Eggleston calls attention to scenes most people overlook

The color photographs of William Eggleston provoke extreme responses. A casual observer might feel that his intensely real images of everyday objects are little more than well-composed, skillfully printed backyard snapshots. Others think that Eggleston is a pace-setting artist showing a photographically new and different view of the world.

In 1975, Eggleston's controversial work was on display at Harvard's Carpenter Center for the Visual Arts. Twenty large prints turned the center's austere glassed-in lobby into a thicket of color, startling passersby on Cambridge's Quincy Street who could view them from outside.

What stopped traffic—and started critics arguing—is not Eggleston's snapshot-like subject matter. That minor battle has been won in the past decade by photographers who have elevated such images into a persuasive documentary art. But those photographers have always worked in black and white, feeling that the lush romantic quality that color seems to impart would interfere with the graphic reality that they wish to capture. William Eggleston shoots his pictures emphatically in color; however, he uses the rich tones not to romanticize his images but to exaggerate their reality—to make their commonplace subjects dramatic.

All of the photographs in the exhibit were taken in and around Memphis, Tennessee—where Eggleston was born in 1939 and still lives—but they show a workaday world that could be just off the highway in any part of the United States. The scenes range from a radiant orange sign for used tires, propped against a heap of them in a filling station *(page 60),* to a neat but undistinguished stucco and brick bungalow in an older suburb *(page 63).* All are images from a bypassed world. It is a world that looks lived in, but there are no people in it, giving the feeling that it has just been abandoned.

The almost tangible reality of these images also gives some viewers the uneasy feeling that they are being hoodwinked by a virtuoso who makes pictures appear too lifelike. Eggleston creates this impression by keeping his prints crisp, vibrant—and sometimes life-sized. He uses expensive dye-transfer prints, which provide both the deepest tones and sharpest definition obtainable in color. Even though the pictures are enlarged 16 times from 35mm transparencies, they have a clarity that can make a dirty pickup truck in an empty lot *(opposite)* seem to jut out of the paper it is reproduced on. In his shot of a jumble of shoes under a tatty bed *(page 58),* the illusion of reality is so strong that the compulsively neat viewer feels compelled to tidy up.

The Major Shows/**Eggleston's Living Color**

The Major Shows/**Eggleston's Living Color**

The Major Shows/**Eggleston's Living Color**

The Major Shows

Edward Weston — A Troubled Master

A retrospective in New York challenges the carefully structured self-image of a pioneer in graphic realism

by Gene Thornton

> Gene Thornton is photography critic for *The New York Times* and a contributing editor of *Art News*. He is currently organizing a major exhibition on 20th Century American photography.

The late Edward Weston's monumental close-ups of sea shells, vegetables, rocks and roots are considered to be among the masterpieces of modern art. These simple still lifes, in which a small and apparently insignificant part of nature achieves the mysterious presence of an ancient stone carving, taught 20th Century photographers to look at subject matter with an eye for abstract form. Like Picasso's Cubist paintings, they outraged many of Weston's contemporaries while making earlier ways of working seem obsolete to others. By now they are so well established that it is hard to remember what photography was like before them.

There is, however, a great deal more to Edward Weston's work than these classic still lifes. One of the virtues of the recent Weston retrospective at The Museum of Modern Art in New York City was that it displayed almost (but not quite) the full range of his achievement. The 264-print exhibition, the first large-scale showing of Weston's photographs in 25 years, also included prime examples of his nudes, landscapes and noncommercial portraits, omitting only the commercial portraits and Salon photographs of his earliest period.

The exhibition also raised again the long-standing question of what Weston's photographs actually mean. The photographer himself always claimed that his best works were purely and simply studies in form. However, both old friends and recent critical writers insist on seeing Weston's pictures as an expression of his deepest feelings about life and love. A fresh look at Weston's own life and his work suggests that there may well have been aspects not only of his photographs, but also of his personality reflected in them, that Weston could never fully discern.

There was no hint of complexity either in Weston's early life or his first photographs. Born into a middle-class professional family near Chicago in 1886, he became an instant devotee of photography at age 16, when his father gave him a Bull's Eye No. 2 camera. At 20 he went to visit his married sister in the quiet country town of Tropico in Southern California, and began his professional career there as a door-to-door portrait photographer. In 1908 he returned for six months to Illinois for his only formal training in the field at the Illinois College of Photography.

He then settled in Tropico, married a friend of his sister's and, after two years of working as a printer for commercial portrait photographers, he opened his own studio. His highly retouched and extremely flattering portraits soon attracted clients from the growing movie colony in nearby Hollywood. As Tropico, later renamed Glendale, grew and was absorbed into greater Los Angeles, Weston built a stable and reasonably lucrative studio business to which he seemed committed indefinitely.

He was, however, soon discontented with the routine of a portrait studio, and in his spare time he began to do landscapes and figure studies, which he

In 1924, Edward Weston and the Italian-born actress and sometime photographer Tina Modotti had this portrait made—in a studio complete with painted backdrop and bouquet of flowers—as if they were a middle-class couple celebrating an anniversary. In fact, Weston had given up his home and family in suburban California to live with Modotti in Mexico City.

sent off to the popular photography magazines and exhibitions that had begun to flourish before the First World War. This skillful but still conventional work won him a solid reputation in the field while he was still in his twenties.

During these years Weston continued to live the quiet life of a respectable professional man. His wife, Flora MacDonald Chandler, came from a family that owned land in what is now greater Los Angeles, and that has since grown very rich. Between 1910 and 1919 Flora bore him four sons, and much of his early artistic success has been attributed to the stabilizing influence of Flora and the children.

But Weston was not cut out for family life. In the deepest core of his being there was a passionate desire for solitude. As a boy in suburban Chicago he had been happiest alone with his camera, and later in life he rose early to have a few precious hours to himself before his household and the business affairs of his portrait studio crowded in on him. Though he loved his children, he could not cope with their day-to-day demands. Even before the birth of his youngest son he had begun moving out of the family circle to spend time with a bohemian group of Southern Californian artists and writers.

Weston was dazzled by his new friends, who "*did* open up new channels, started me thinking from many fresh angles, looking toward hitherto unconsidered horizons." Under their tutelage he adopted in his personal work the soft-focus approach of the Pictorial photographers who, following the precepts and example of the American painter James McNeill Whistler, played down human interest and storytelling in favor of emphasis on design, color and tone. From here to true abstraction was an easy step, and Weston took it in the 1920s, when European artists such as Matisse, Picasso and Brancusi replaced Whistler as the idols of the American avant-garde.

Weston's gradual but decisive development as a photographer was paralleled by his growing dissatisfaction with married life in suburban Glendale. While continuing to earn a living at portraiture, he began to keep diaries (or "daybooks," as he preferred to call them) which he filled with contemptuous references to "drab, gray Glendale" and its "hustle, bustle, meddle, push." Increasingly he was caught up in the late parties and casual couplings among his bohemian friends. Then, in the early '20s, he met a beautiful young Italian-born movie starlet who aspired to a larger life as a photographer and intellectual. Tina Modotti became his pupil and lover, and in 1923, at the age of 37, Weston shut up his studio in drab, gray Glendale and went off with Tina on a trip to Mexico.

This break was not altogether a Gauguinesque escape from the responsibilities of middle-class life, for Weston set up a new portrait studio in a large house in the fashionable Juarez district of Mexico City. Neither was it a purely amorous escapade, for Weston took his 13-year-old eldest son along,

The Major Shows/**Edward Weston**

and Flora, his wife, sent money to help out from time to time. It was not even very much fun. Weston was disturbed by Mexico's poverty and political turmoil, and his love life began to sour. Tina took to Communism—and to a succession of youthful revolutionaries as lovers, while Weston began to sleep with the housemaids. Eventually their affair foundered on mutual infidelity.

But along with its confusions, contradictions and disappointments, the trip to Mexico was clearly a watershed in Weston's life. He began a whole new approach to portraiture. Using a hand-held 3¼ x 4¼ Graflex instead of the 8 x 10 view camera on a tripod that he had previously favored in his studio work, he made a series of stop-motion portraits of Tina and other friends, which were radically different from his carefully posed and retouched commercial portraits. His aim, he said, was to capture "fractions of seconds of emotional intensity." But, along with their spontaneity, these heads achieved a larger-than-life-sized grandeur, more godlike than human.

He took an even more radical approach to nudes. Early 20th Century photographers often cut off the figure at the neck or turned the face away from the camera to protect the anonymity of the model. Weston went much further —and not for modesty's sake. He showed only part of the body, or had the model fold herself into contracted positions, thus putting parts of the body together with other parts to reduce any emotional reaction to the resulting photograph of the nude figure. "Most of the series is entirely impersonal," he wrote of a group of Mexican nudes, "lacking in any human contexts which might call attention to living, palpitating bodies."

By the time Weston ended his Mexican sojourn in 1926 he was a different man. Although he left Tina behind, he did not return to his wife. He moved restlessly, back to Glendale, next to San Francisco and then, disgusted by city life, to the picturesque little holiday town of Carmel, California. Meanwhile he continued to pursue the goal of an impersonal esthetic response to form —with some very odd results.

He began to produce a new genre of monumental close-ups—of shells and vegetables. These heroic representations of tiny and often mundane objects became, in time, his most famous pictures. The subject matter of these pioneering studies was suggested to Weston by Henrietta Shore, a now-forgotten Californian painter. Henry, as she preferred to be called, made meticulously rendered drawings of rocks, shells and roots, which frequently included explicitly erotic shapes. A heavy-set virginal lady, Henry was no longer young when Weston met her, and Weston believed that her suggestive pictures were twisted reflections of the celibate life she had led.

However, he thought that he, with the objectivity of the camera's eye, could see an object as it really was, uncolored by the sort of personal interpretation that Henry practiced. Such an impersonal portrayal, Weston believed,

Henrietta Shore: *Trees*

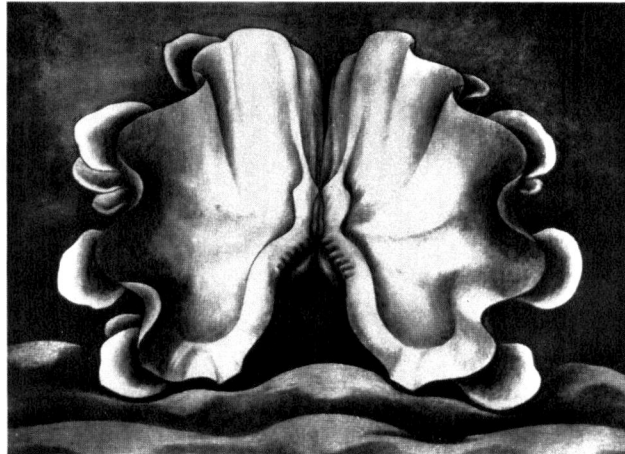

Henrietta Shore: *Shell*

These carefully detailed yet highly stylized drawings of tree trunks and shells by the obscure California artist Henrietta Shore opened Weston's eyes to a new type of subject matter. Though Shore's drawings usually contained erotic overtones, Weston tried to suppress such emotional content from the photographs they inspired. But critics have found suggestive sexual images even in his shells and vegetables.

revealed not only the object, but through it, the whole of creation. "To see a World in a Grain of Sand,/ And a Heaven in a Wild Flower," the poet William Blake had written. This is what Weston wanted to do in his brilliantly detailed studies of shells and vegetables.

To his surprise, however, other people insisted on interpreting these close-ups as disturbing expressions of intensely personal—though possibly unconscious—feelings. When he sent photographs of a chambered nautilus to Tina, with whom he still kept up a correspondence, she wrote back to tell him that she had found the pictures highly erotic. "I cannot look at them long without feeling exceedingly perturbed . . . not only mentally but physically. They contain both the innocence of natural things and the morbidity of a sophisticated, distorted mind."

Weston was puzzled by this response. He continued to insist that personal feelings played no part in his work. "Not once while working with the shells did I have any physical reaction to them; nor did I try to record erotic symbolism. I am not sick and I was never so free from sexual suppression—which if I had, might easily enter into my work."

He had the same experience with his images of vegetables. Describing the photograph called *Pepper No. 30,* which in time became the most celebrated of all his works, he wrote, "It is a pepper, but more than a pepper . . . [it] takes one beyond the world we know into an inner reality—the absolute—with a clear understanding, a mystic revealment."

However, other people insisted on seeing the pepper as a writhing, distorted but very sexy human body. The most Weston would ever concede was that he saw peppers and other natural forms "with such intensity, such direct honesty that a tremendous force like sex, which enters, permeates all nature, could not but be revealed."

The truth would seem to be that Weston could allow his true feelings to emerge only when photographing an indifferent object like a shell or a vegetable, and even then he could not let himself know what he was doing. When he photographed people, even the women he slept with, he was always on guard against human responses.

This detached approach enabled Weston to create a new way of dealing even with such traditional subject matter as landscapes, to which he reapplied himself in 1929. A few miles from the village of Carmel stands a promontory called Point Lobos where wind-twisted cypresses and dramatic confrontations of sky, sea and rocky headland provided Weston's generation of photographers and painters with a reservoir of subject matter that he felt none of his contemporaries recorded properly. "Poor abused cypresses," wrote Weston that same year, "photographed in all their picturesqueness by tourists . . . etched, painted and generally vilified by every self-labeled 'art-

The Major Shows/**Edward Weston**

ist.' " When Weston photographed Point Lobos he zeroed in on details of root and rock or on tangles of kelp drying on the pebbly beach.

By now this abstract approach dominated his treatment of virtually all the subjects he selected—the fantastic rock formations of the Mojave Desert, the towering sand dunes of Oceano on the Pacific Coast, the backside of a favorite model, the spiky desert plants that he preferred to the soft, leafy plants of garden, orchard and field. Each image achieved the bare, austere beauty that was peculiarly Weston's.

Thus, in spite of his avowed efforts to avoid personal interpretation, in spite of his attempts to depict the world with the objectivity of a machine, Weston ended, like all modern artists, by creating a highly personal world of his own. It was a strange but beautiful world in which nature was filled with fragments of human feeling while human beings were often reduced to abstract designs, a world in which people and peppers seemed to interchange.

The striking and idiosyncratic style of Weston's work seized the attention of other artists and patrons of photography far beyond the limits of Carmel and Southern California. In 1930, Weston held a New York showing—his first in that city, which even then was center stage for the display of photographic work. The New York show was followed by other exhibits in Boston, Chicago and San Francisco. For the first time, too, his personally motivated work began to pay for itself, and soon made more money than did his commercial portraiture. Finally, in 1937, he became the first photographer ever to win a John Simon Guggenheim Memorial Fellowship, a $2,000 award that helped him give up the commercial portraiture he had come to loathe, and devote himself full time to work of his own choosing.

Weston's winning of photography's first Guggenheim Fellowship was a joyous climax to his life and career. He had recently entered into a love affair with Charis Wilson, a beautiful woman nearly 30 years his junior who later became his second wife. His son Neil soon built them, in the woods near Point Lobos, the simple, isolated cottage Weston had long wanted to live in. As a popular novelette the life and work of Weston could end right here, with success achieved and prospects of joy ahead.

In fact, however, the freedom to work full time with a beautiful, loving young woman as his assistant did not result in the complete self-realization that might have been expected. The severe, objective approach that had brought Weston fame and prosperity began to give way to what has been described, even by so ardent a partisan as John Szarkowski, director of the Department of Photography at The Museum of Modern Art and codirector with Willard Van Dyke of the Weston retrospective, as a "more casual, more natural, and somehow less *artistic*" approach. Farmland and flowers began to appear in Weston's landscape photographs, along with quaint old buildings

EDWARD WESTON: *Pepper No. 30,* 1930

Weston's most renowned photograph is this close-up of a garden pepper. To him the convoluted form and glossy surfaces revealed in microcosm the essence of the natural world, but others saw it as an expression of Weston's fiercely sensual inner self.

and icicles glittering in the sunlight. At times he seemed almost to flirt with the picturesque.

Szarkowski defends this development on balance as a consolidation and advance over Weston's earlier work. Though these later landscapes appear more relaxed, Szarkowski says, they are really "more complex, more subtle . . . more difficult and more sophisticated." However, Janet Malcolm, photography critic for *The New Yorker* magazine, condemns them as "a kind of Sierra Club Realism . . . which represent a reversion to early photography rather than a development of the medium," and her view may well prevail.

Weston never did recover the austere vision of his classic still lifes. It was as if his love for Charis had brought him out of his essential solitude without giving him a new basis for art.

By 1946 the years had begun to overtake Weston. He was 60 and not well, and his 12 remaining years were a mixture of triumph and tragedy. The themes and approaches he had pioneered in the 1920s and '30s were now being widely imitated by both professionals and the serious amateurs of camera clubs. His commanding position among modern photographers was solidified by a big retrospective exhibition at The Museum of Modern Art. Henceforward, virtually nothing that he did could be wrong, but by this time his artistic strength was failing and his personal life was a wreck. His young wife, Charis, had left him, and he learned in 1947 that he had Parkinson's disease, a paralyzing degeneration of the nervous system, from which he was to die in 1958.

Alone once again and face to face with death, knowing that he would soon be unable to work, he took his camera to Point Lobos and turned it, not on the kelp, the pebbles and the sea, which he had so often photographed in closeup before, but on the grand panorama of dying cypresses and stone cliffs out of which masses of wild flowers erupted in spring. These brooding landscapes with their dark intimations of mortality are among the most beautiful pictures Weston ever took, and in them he seems, for the first time in his career, to have uttered cries of anguish directly from the heart.

The Major Shows/**Edward Weston**

A Passion for Form

Ramiel in His Attic, 1920

The late Edward Weston's special talent for depicting a subject's essential form called for a photographic technique that would yield, as he put it, "first conceptions coming straight through unadulterated."

The instrument he most relied upon was a sturdy 8 x 10 view camera. Early in his career—beginning about 1914—he used it with soft-focus lenses to capture hazily lit figures like the dappled nude at right. Later, in the '20s, he photographed his subjects under an even light with a lens he had bought in Mexico for five dollars. Stopping it down to a pinhole aperture, Weston made exposures of up to five hours to create his momentous still lifes, such as Chambered Nautilus *(page 75).*

Striving for greater definition in the '30s *(page 74),* Weston shot nudes, against dark backgrounds, with a 4 x 5 Graflex, limiting exposures to two minutes or less. But for a heroic portrait, like that on page 73, he exposed under a second, using a hand-held 3¼ x 4¼ Graflex. Except for a smaller-format picture like this, Weston seldom enlarged his negatives, but printed them in their original size.

He stuck to these simple classic formulas throughout his life. Even in his final years, during the mid-'40s, he continued to haul the unwieldy 8 x 10 camera out to Point Lobos, California. There, Weston and his camera still rendered "more clearly than the eyes see" the unique world that he alone was able to define.

Reflected Sunlight on Torso, 1922

The Major Shows/**Edward Weston**

Hands against Kimono, 1924

José Clemente Orozco, 1930

The Major Shows/**Edward Weston**

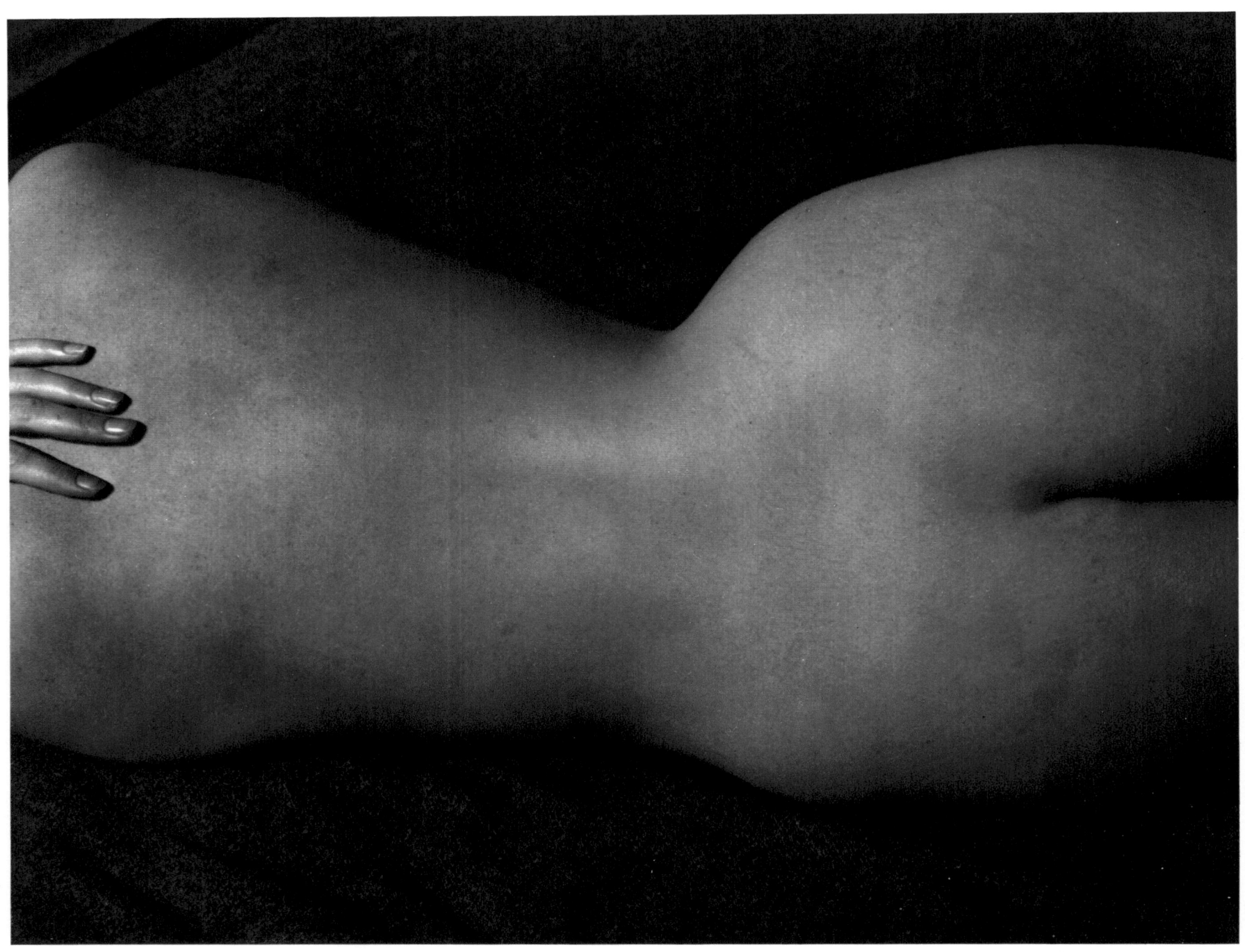

Nude, 1935

Chambered Nautilus, 1927

The Major Shows/**Edward Weston**

Oak, Monterey County, 1929

Surf, China Cove, 1938

The Major Shows/**Edward Weston**

Nude on Sand, 1936

Tomato Field, Monterey Coast, 1937

The Major Shows/**Edward Weston**

Point Lobos, 1946

Discoveries/3

Discoveries / 3

A Global Search	84
Artful Synthesizer	86
A Dream Revisited	92
Images of Time	100
A Floating World	106
Darkroom Ghosts	112

JAMES HENKEL

ANTONÍN NOVÝ

JURAJ LIPTÁK

ROBERT MAY

SHIN YANAGISAWA

Discoveries

A Global Search for New Talent

From a field of 55 entries nominated by an international panel, five promising photographers have been singled out by the Editors for special recognition

Each year the Editors of PHOTOGRAPHY YEAR search all over the world to find talented new photographers who have not yet received the recognition they deserve. To arrive at their choices of the field's most gifted newcomers, the Editors consult with an international panel of celebrated photographers, teachers, curators and editors, whose expert knowledge of local photography covers significant portions of Asia, Latin America, Eastern and Western Europe and both coasts of North America. The six consultants this year are: photographer Manuel Alvarez Bravo of Mexico, whose pictures have been exhibited from Moscow to Manhattan; Anna Farova, Curator of the National Collection of Photographs at Prague; Harold Jones, head of the Department of Photography at the University of Arizona in Tucson; Joan Murray, photography editor of *Artweek* magazine; Akira Okami, editor of *Asahi Camera* in Japan; and Jean-Maurice Rouquette, Director of the Musée Réattu at Arles, France, home of one of Europe's leading photography collections.

Each consultant was invited to nominate up to 10 photographers whose work had not yet been granted an important forum or received a major award. In general, the nominees had become known to the panel members only within the past few years. Although any of the nominees may have had individual pictures published or shown in museums or galleries, none of them has had a major book or exhibition. And unlike the qualifications for other photographic awards, this PHOTOGRAPHY YEAR competition welcomed every type of subject, every technique, every style—so long as the primary element was in some way photographic. The panel of consultants submitted the names of 55 photographers from five countries. Then the Editors wrote each photographer directly to ask for a portfolio of 25 pictures. As they arrived, the portfolios were carefully studied.

In each of the past three years, this sifting process had uncovered some surprising but very marked consistencies in the work submitted by the various photographers. In 1972, the influence of documentary photography was pervasive; esthetics was the preoccupation the next year; color photography dominated the next. What tied the photographers together this year was their tendency to make intensely personal statements.

This subjective approach is particularly striking in the work of the five photographers who were finally chosen. Two are from Czechoslovakia, two from the American South and one from Japan. Interestingly, the sense of privacy that distinguished this year's nominees is nowhere more intensely felt than in the work of the two photographers from behind the Iron Curtain, where state doctrine might have been expected to encourage a more realistic—or more conformist—viewpoint. The fact is that each of these young men, like their colleagues, has used photography as an extension of—and voice for—a highly interesting self.

THE PHOTOGRAPHY YEAR
Panel of Consultants

Top row, left to right

AKIRA OKAMI
Editor of *Asahi Camera*, Tokyo

ANNA FAROVA
Curator of the National Collection
of Photographs,
Prague, Czechoslovakia

Middle row, left to right

MANUEL ALVAREZ BRAVO
Photographer, Mexico City

JOAN MURRAY
Photography Editor of *Artweek*
magazine, Oakland, California

Bottom row, left to right

HAROLD JONES
Chairman of the Photography Department,
University of Arizona, Tucson, Arizona

JEAN-MAURICE ROUQUETTE
Curator of the Musée Réattu,
Arles, France

Photographers nominated by the consultants

Denis Barrau, Mouries, France
Jean-Marc Bustamante, Toulouse, France
Jo An Callis, Los Angeles
Mark Cohen, Wilkes-Barre, Pennsylvania
Steve Collins, San Francisco
Carlos Azpieta Conde, Coyodcan, Mexico
Bernard Descamps, Gagny, France
John Divola, Venice, California
Gérard Fraissenet, Arles, France
Carlos Blanco Fuentes, Mexico City
Lazáro Blanco Fuentes, Mexico City
Serge Gal, Clarensac, France
Jan Groover, New York City
*James Henkel, Penland, North Carolina
Jim Hill, Half Moon Bay, California
Graciela Iturbide, Mexico City
Chris Johnson, San Francisco
Bishin Jumonji, Tokyo
Nakahisa Kimura, Shizuoka City, Japan
Akira Kinoshita, Yokohama City, Japan
Roland Laboye, Castres, France
Brigitte Langevin, Versailles, France
Pauline Lavista, Mexico City
Rafael Donis Lechón, Mexico City
*Juraj Lipták, Bratislava, Czechoslovakia
Milota Marková-Havránková, Bratislava, Czechoslovakia

Michael Massi, Toulon, France
Robert Mautner, Canoga Park, California
*Robert May, Lexington, Kentucky
Emila Medková, Prague
Yoshikazu Minami, Saitama, Japan
Virgil Mirano, Los Angeles
Ichiro Morita, Tokyo
John McWilliams, Atlanta
Yuji Nakagawa, Hokkaido, Japan
Alois Nožická, Prague
*Antonín Nový, Prague
Yoshino Oishi, Tokyo
G. Lee Phillips, Claremont, California
Leland Rice, Los Angeles
José Angel Rodríguez, Mexico City
Kathryn Schooley-Robbins, Tucson, Arizona
Jan Svoboda, Prague
Jacqueline Thurston, Menlo Park, California
Karen Truax, Albuquerque, New Mexico
Marc Tulane, Menerbes, France
Antonio Turok, Mexico City
Colette Urbajtel, Mexico City
Jesús Sanchez Uribe, Mexico City
Josef Vásă, Prague
Hitomi Wanatabe, Tokyo
*Shin Yanagisawa, Tokyo
Peter Zhoř, Prague

* *Work of this photographer is shown on the following pages.*

Discoveries

James Henkel—An Artful Synthesizer

A young photography instructor tears, paints and pastes his pictures to produce highly personal, multicolored images

What the 28-year-old interpretive photographer James Henkel does to a photograph shouldn't happen to a comic valentine. He tears it, he scribbles on it, he pastes it down with other pictures to produce a work which, ultimately, is not so much photography as a mélange dominated by a photograph. In one such work, *Letter from Camp (right)*, the principal image is an Instamatic snapshot, taken by a friend, of the photographer dressed for volleyball. This picture has been superimposed on a brown print of palm trees, which in turn has been placed on top of a sheet of paper torn from a spiral bound notebook. The photographer has worked over these various elements with watercolor washes, colored pencils and crayons. Though the hint of sports and outdoor life suggests the kind of news a letter from camp might include, the montage includes no actual letter from camp.

The overall result of this composite technique is a sequence of sometimes cryptic images that Henkel uses to record his deepest feelings. Oddly, the original photographs are taken almost at random. "I don't go out with my camera on planned picture-taking trips," Henkel says. "I use the camera to collect information which I'm intrigued with, and then I deal with the images after they're printed—drawing, tearing, manipulating them—to get at the qualities which originally impelled me to make the exposure. The pictures are just day-to-day stuff, taken wherever I happened to be."

Henkel did not start out to be a photographer at all, much less an innovator. Born in Lancaster, Pennsylvania, in 1947 and raised in Miami, Florida, his ambition was to become a painter. But at Florida State University, he increasingly fell under the influence of one of his instructors, photographer-artist Timo Tauno Pajunen, and ended by receiving a Master of Fine Arts degree in photography in 1974. Henkel himself has since become an instructor of photography at The Penland School in Penland, North Carolina, where he has the opportunity to share his extraordinary perceptions—and techniques—with his students.

There is a surrealist quality to Henkel's use of chance to get at his own basic reactions to things. There is also a surrealist aspect to his method of juxtaposing seemingly unrelated images or transforming simple images into something more complex and suggestive. In the portfolio of Henkel's photographs which continues overleaf, clouds appear where there are none, a flower patch seems to stretch toward infinity, and color is added and subtracted at will. None of these devices are designed to confuse, but rather to make richer the viewer's innate perceptions of ordinary things. This, in fact, is the heart of the young photographer's purpose. Dissatisfied with the more literal aspects of the photographic image, Henkel goes to great pains to alter what has been recorded so that the new image will correspond more accurately with a subjective response.

Letter from Camp, December 1974

Discoveries/**James Henkel**

Untitled, April 1975

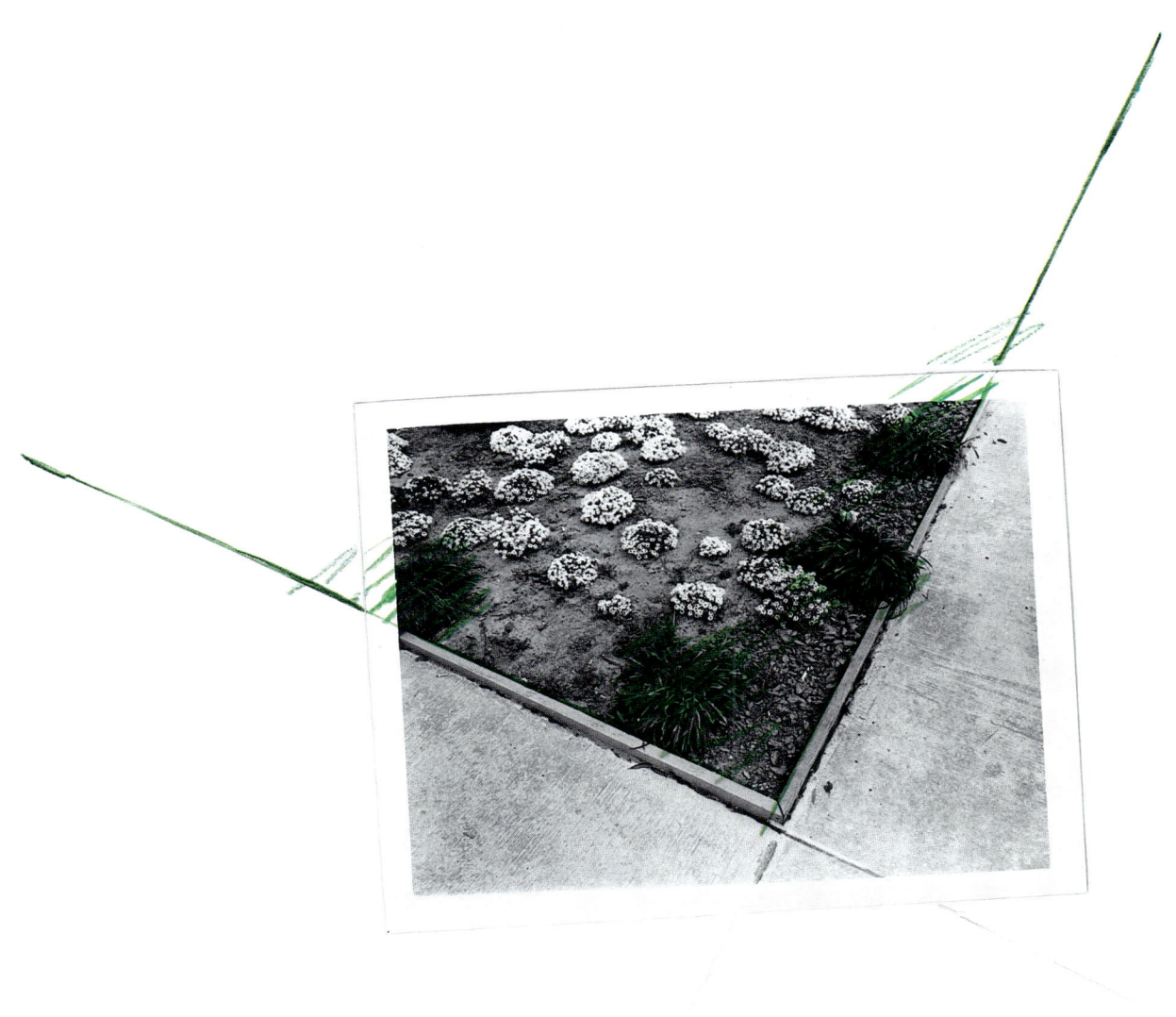

Untitled, April 1975

Discoveries/**James Henkel**

Untitled, February 1975

Aerial Section, January 1975

Discoveries

Antonín Nový – The Sensual Past

A former steelworker's seductive pictures of young girls in a fin-de-siècle painter's house evoke the lush and colorful atmosphere of bohemian Europe

Swathed in diaphanous veils or offered nude to the camera's eye, the voluptuous young women at right and on the following pages lie dreamy-eyed —or move toward the viewer—amid tapestries, pillows and paintings that belong to some other time and place. They are dream girls made only for love, and Czech photographer Antonín Nový has presented them as an old dream, brought back to life by his own romantic and imaginative concepts.

"I consider photography a means of linking the past with the present," Nový says, "of linking emotional relics with the present moment." And his photographs of girls, all made in the past two years, indeed create links with the artistic life of the Continent during the end of the 19th Century. They were inspired by the girls rendered in the work of the turn-of-the-century Czechoslovakian painter and poster designer Alphonse Mucha, whose decorative Art Nouveau posters of famous actresses like Sarah Bernhardt still adorn the dormitory rooms of a few American college students.

Paradoxically, Nový's dreamlike pictures were made in a nation whose doctrine encourages artists to depict the conflicts and struggles of everyday life in an affirmative and realistic style. Nový's art, however, flourishes in spite of —or perhaps in protest against—official sponsorship of socialist realism. (Other examples of this kind of art from Czechoslovakia are represented in the photographs of Juraj Lipták on pages 112 to 118 and of Josef Koudelka on pages 188 to 195.)

Novy has lived most of his life under this regime. Born in Prague in 1944, 12 years before the Communist takeover of Czechoslovakia, Nový was a 19-year-old steelworker when he made his first photographs with a borrowed camera. After his marriage in 1966, he managed to acquire a job as wirephoto operator and picture editor with the Czechoslovakian news agency, Ceteka. Since then he has made his living as a documentary-film cameraman and news photographer.

The studies of girls were made in his leisure time, with a hand-held 35mm camera, and have never before been published or even shown except to a small circle of friends, mostly poets, "to pay back my debt for having read their works." Despite their mature and worldly appearance, his models were high school students. Once the background and draperies were chosen he encouraged them to move around freely and find their own poses.

"When I worked as a news photographer, I myself was only a witness," he says. "Now I am trying to be a partner and create a quiet dialogue with beauty and harmony, as represented by the female body." The dreamlike quality of his pictures springs from this deeply romantic approach. "Photography should be something festive and therefore a remedy against the common grayness," Nový says. The haunting, evocative photographs presented here. are a dramatic realization of that intention.

Aerial Section, January 1975

Discoveries

Antonín Nový —The Sensual Past

A former steelworker's seductive pictures of young girls in a fin-de-siècle painter's house evoke the lush and colorful atmosphere of bohemian Europe

Swathed in diaphanous veils or offered nude to the camera's eye, the voluptuous young women at right and on the following pages lie dreamy-eyed —or move toward the viewer—amid tapestries, pillows and paintings that belong to some other time and place. They are dream girls made only for love, and Czech photographer Antonín Nový has presented them as an old dream, brought back to life by his own romantic and imaginative concepts.

"I consider photography a means of linking the past with the present," Nový says, "of linking emotional relics with the present moment." And his photographs of girls, all made in the past two years, indeed create links with the artistic life of the Continent during the end of the 19th Century. They were inspired by the girls rendered in the work of the turn-of-the-century Czechoslovakian painter and poster designer Alphonse Mucha, whose decorative Art Nouveau posters of famous actresses like Sarah Bernhardt still adorn the dormitory rooms of a few American college students.

Paradoxically, Nový's dreamlike pictures were made in a nation whose doctrine encourages artists to depict the conflicts and struggles of everyday life in an affirmative and realistic style. Nový's art, however, flourishes in spite of —or perhaps in protest against—official sponsorship of socialist realism. (Other examples of this kind of art from Czechoslovakia are represented in the photographs of Juraj Lipták on pages 112 to 118 and of Josef Koudelka on pages 188 to 195.)

Novy has lived most of his life under this regime. Born in Prague in 1944, 12 years before the Communist takeover of Czechoslovakia, Nový was a 19-year-old steelworker when he made his first photographs with a borrowed camera. After his marriage in 1966, he managed to acquire a job as wirephoto operator and picture editor with the Czechoslovakian news agency, Ceteka. Since then he has made his living as a documentary-film cameraman and news photographer.

The studies of girls were made in his leisure time, with a hand-held 35mm camera, and have never before been published or even shown except to a small circle of friends, mostly poets, "to pay back my debt for having read their works." Despite their mature and worldly appearance, his models were high school students. Once the background and draperies were chosen he encouraged them to move around freely and find their own poses.

"When I worked as a news photographer, I myself was only a witness," he says. "Now I am trying to be a partner and create a quiet dialogue with beauty and harmony, as represented by the female body." The dreamlike quality of his pictures springs from this deeply romantic approach. "Photography should be something festive and therefore a remedy against the common grayness," Nový says. The haunting, evocative photographs presented here are a dramatic realization of that intention.

Antonín Nový's photographs on this and the following six pages were inspired by—and photographed in the apartment of—the-turn-of-the-century Czech artist, Alphonse Mucha.

Discoveries / **Antonín Nový**

Discoveries / **Antonín Nový**

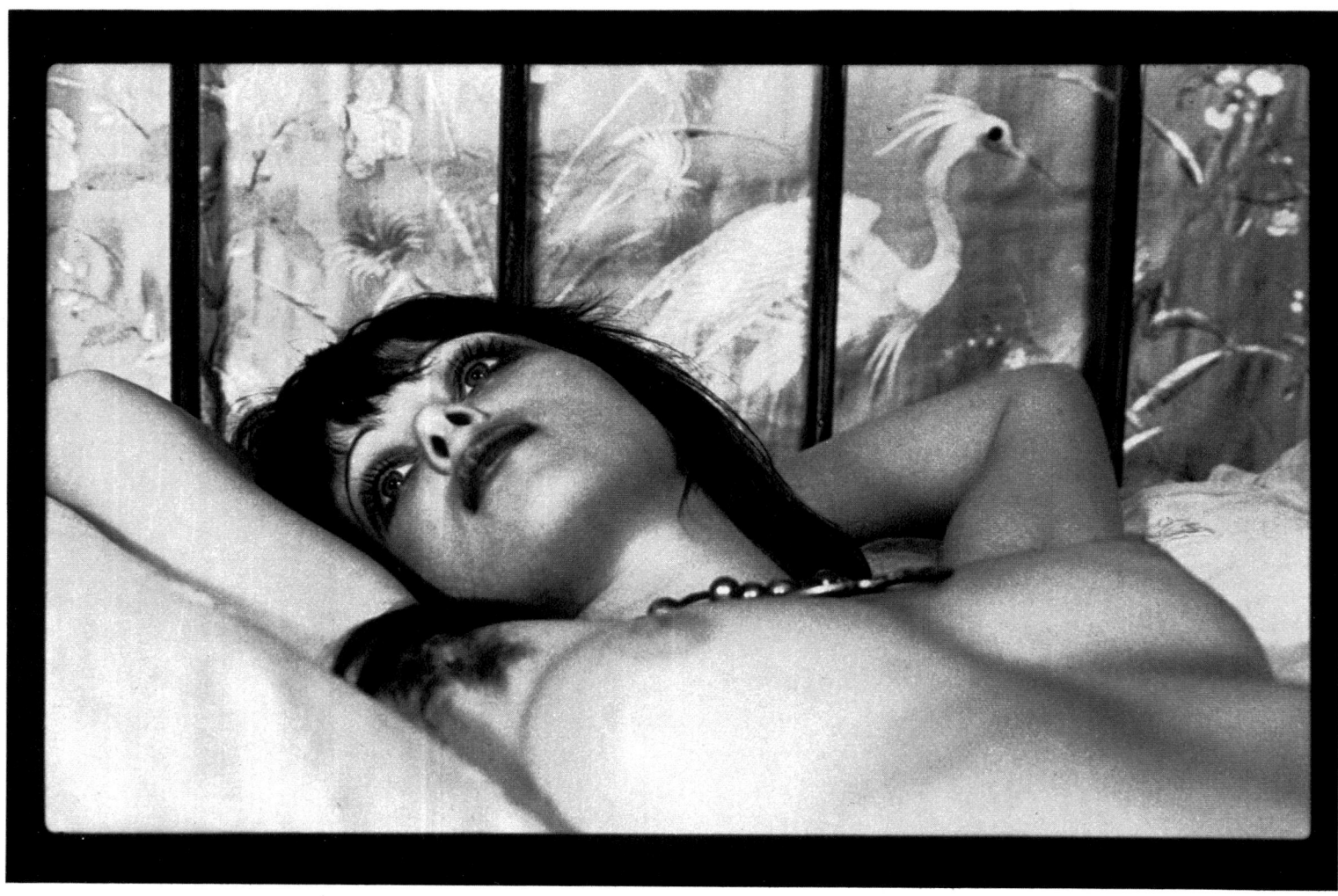

Discoveries / **Antonín Nový**

Discoveries

Robert May —The Flow of Time

The blurred images and double exposures of a Kentucky weekend photographer convey an impression of change in an apparently unchanging world

There is always something disturbingly complex and out of focus in Robert May's photographs of simple country scenes. His camera has moved and the image has also moved and multiplied. Cows peacefully graze beside a pond —and behind or above the ghosts of other peacefully grazing cows. As an old shed seems to totter and collapse, a burst of light streaks outward from the center of the picture, and the shed dissolves into cornstalks silhouetted against the sky. The sunlit trees rise steeply up a hillside and mutate into thousands of scintillating points, as if growing before the viewer's eyes.

At first glance the double exposures and blurry images may merely seem inept, the unintended result of the photographer's hand moving just at the moment of exposure. With Robert May, however, the results are meticulously calculated. He calls his double exposures "in-camera multiples," and he uses this seemingly accidental device to create his own world of evolving reality. "The old farm shed leans slightly," he explains. "By creating movement with a double exposure I suggest the feeling of a process of decay or of slowly slipping away that may not be actually perceptible except over a long period of time." Similarly, the multiple outlines of leaves suggest the growth that is actually too slow for the eye to capture. As the pictures accumulate, they indeed add up to a quiet but compelling vision of a changing world where a suggestion of the future has been visualized.

May's world of private perceptions is deeply rooted in the real world around him. He has lived in Lexington, Kentucky, a small Southern city in the heart of an old agricultural region, since his birth in 1935 and today works there as an audio-visual specialist for a large corporation. "This is," he says, "the area that I best know, understand and love." He began photographing it at the age of 13 and came to his practice of double exposure only after years of more conventional photography. In 1948 he joined the Lexington Camera Club where he met Van Derek Coke, who became the director of the George Eastman House in Rochester, New York and the late Ralph Eugene Meatyard, already known for his enigmatic photographs of local subjects. Later he studied with both men, and attended a summer workshop given by the photographer-teacher Minor White.

Unlike most regional photographers he learned to eschew the obviously beautiful or picturesque for quiet, ordinary scenes that speak more to the native. He works slowly and patiently to come to a deeper understanding of his chosen subject. On a typical weekend he rises early and drives out to the countryside on old back roads. He enjoys "talking to the farmers or visiting country stores around lunchtime." But most of his time is spent "exploring, looking, feeling and waiting" for the moment when everything comes together for a picture. Only when he senses the evolution of time in his lens, does he trip the shutter.

Discoveries/**Robert May**

Discoveries/**Robert May**

Discoveries

Shin Yanagisawa —The New Japan

Candid shots of revelry under Kyoto's cherry trees provide insights into the mingling of Oriental tradition and modern Western life style

Although born and raised in Japan, Shin Yanagisawa was as surprised as any foreigner might have been by the "chaos and riotous revelry of drunken people" that he found one Sunday night in April under the flowering cherry trees of Kyoto. Kyoto is an ancient city of temples, palaces and gardens, and like most Japanese, Yanagisawa had the impression that the people of Kyoto were gentle and quiet. However, the bacchanalian reality he discovered that April night was so "intriguing," he says, "that I shot away like mad." The result, which Yanagisawa calls *The Night Cherry Blossoms of Kyoto,* is a strikingly modern study of Japanese students and workers celebrating the traditional rites of cherry-blossom time.

A good-natured spirit pervades these shot-from-the-hip candid pictures. Under the flowering trees of the Maruyama Park, musicians stroll. A group of students *(page 108)* play a Japanese game called Jan Ken Pon (paper, rock and scissors); the loser of each round must take off an article of clothing—as in American strip poker. Amid the fun, Yanagisawa also noticed other cross-cultural paradoxes typical of Japanese life today. In one photograph *(opposite)* a group of weavers clowns for the camera. When at work at their looms they make *nishijin,* a traditional type of elaborate silk brocade, but on this holiday night they are wearing Western suits and striped ties. Musicians in Japanese sandals and kimonos provide a traditional setting, but they smoke Western cigarettes and make their way across a litter of empty cigarette packages and abandoned newspapers.

Like some of the subjects in his Kyoto pictures, Yanagisawa is himself caught between two worlds. The product of a middle-class Japanese upbringing (his father is a doctor), Yanagisawa attended the Tokyo Photography College between 1953 and 1957. While a student there, he first heard the names of the photographers who were to influence him most decisively: Europeans like Eugène Atget, Bill Brandt, Robert Frank; the Americans Walker Evans and Harry Callahan. After graduation he became a freelance photographer. Though untraveled outside Japan, Yanagisawa has made a point of keeping up with developments in photography in other countries.

Both in the way he handles his camera to capture significant fragments of everyday life, and in his exclusive use of black-and-white film, Yanagisawa clearly has a place in the documentary tradition which descends from his Western photographic heroes. However, his Kyoto pictures also relate to the traditional Japanese art of such 18th and 19th Century woodcut masters as Hiroshige and Utamara, who recorded what was then called the "floating world" of working-class pleasures and festivals with snapshot clarity and casualness. Thus Yanagisawa has drawn on the expressive elements of both traditional Japanese and modern Western culture to produce an intriguing version of his own floating world of contemporary Japanese life.

Revelers at a Summer Party, Kyoto

Discoveries/**Shin Yanagisawa**

Students Playing Stripping Game

Strolling Musicians Tuning Instruments

Discoveries/**Shin Yanagisawa**

Strolling Musician Seeking Customers

Man Overcome by Rice Wine

Discoveries

Juraj Lipták — Ghosts from the Darkroom

An innovative Czech uses printing techniques to overlay homely subjects with an aura of mystery

A ghostly presence constantly tries to assert itself in the cryptic, haunting photographs of Juraj Lipták. The ostensible subject matter is commonplace enough: a window, a cloud, a sun-streaked forest, a library table littered with odds and ends, a hand. But somewhere between the subject matter and the finished picture—like a poltergeist in a living room on a placid summer Sunday afternoon—something enters to disturb the peace. It may be a whirling jiggle of light on the negative. It may be an eccentric bit of framing that seems somehow to just miss getting the ostensible subject matter properly placed. It may be a sepia-toned photograph within a black-and-white photograph, suggesting worlds within worlds. Of this latter practice, one of his favorites, Lipták says, "Since the beginning I have tried to make use of the illusory space of photos within photos." But whatever Lipták's device may be—and it changes from picture to picture—it is a signal that there is more in the photograph than a casual glance will discern.

Lipták does not often talk about the meaning of his photographs. He prefers to speak matter-of-factly about photographic paper and darkroom procedures, or of the ways in which different colors relate. However, his photographs are clearly part of the great outburst of bizarre and subjective art that has occurred recently in Eastern Europe.

A 27-year-old native of Czechoslovakia, Lipták received an education in photography at the Vocational High School of Applied Arts in the provincial city of Bratislava, and after graduation worked first as a camera assistant, then as a photographer, for television. He spent four years in Prague studying art photography at the FAMU/Film Academy, before going back to Bratislava, where he now lives and works as a photo-reporter.

Lipták is conscious of the rich Czechoslovakian tradition of art photography, and he acknowledges the influence of Josef Sudek, whose atmospheric studies of Prague cityscapes and gardens have influenced a whole generation of younger photographers. In fact, Lipták's current project—to photograph the suburbs of Bratislava before they are torn down—is reminiscent of Sudek's own study of suburban Prague. But his work is also flavored by his admiration for the disturbing portraits of the late American photographer Diane Arbus and by the grisly war reportage of the British photojournalist Don McCullin.

Shooting mostly in black and white with both large and small format cameras and lenses ranging from 20 to 135mm, Lipták uses the camera as only the first step in the picture-making process. It is in the darkroom where the magic is applied—in sepia toning, choice of paper, the flicking on of a light and other subtleties of darkroom manipulation. In other hands, such effects might be mere tricks; in Lipták's, they help bring about a sense of not quite visible presences in his pictures.

Memories of M

Discoveries/**Juraj Lipták**

Window 2

Window 3

Discoveries/**Juraj Lipták**

Big Cloud

Landscape

Discoveries/**Juraj Lipták**

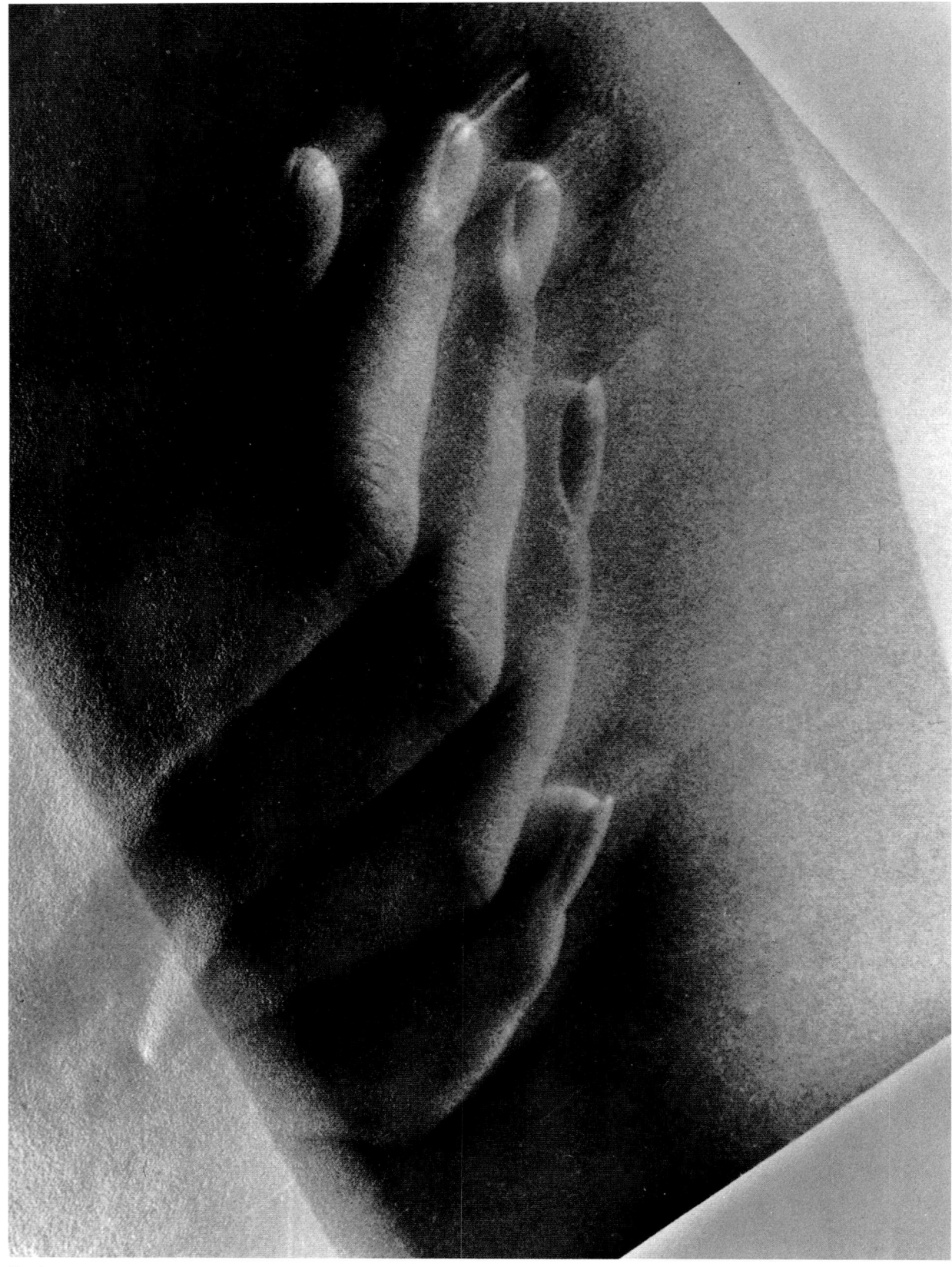

Morning

Assignment/4

Assignment /4

| The Presidency | 122 |

The Presidency / DAVID HUME KENNERLY: *Gerald Ford Looking Down on the Washington Monument from His Helicopter,* 1974

Assignment

Ford by Kennerly: A Bold New View of the Presidency

A photographer's special relationship with the President produces a fresh perspective on America's highest office

When Gerald Ford stepped onto the balcony of the White House on August 11, 1974, two days after being sworn in as President, and waved to the press photographers assembled below, he was suddenly joined by a bearded young man who energetically mimicked his greeting. If the photographers were surprised by the grandstanding, they were not at all mystified about who was doing it. David Hume Kennerly had only recently been one of them. Now, as the "personal photographer to the President," Kennerly was in a position to live the dream of many a professional photojournalist: to make candid, unrehearsed photographs in the White House.

Kennerly's unique opportunity has resulted in photographs that are as historically important as they are dramatic. Offering the first intimate view of an incumbent American President and his advisors, they bequeath to posterity an unprecedented record of the daily work of men making decisions that affect much of the world. Nothing like this collection of scenes has ever been available before. Such a record, of course, might have been made by any photographer given unlimited entrée. Kennerly has done more, for his pictures reflect his own high qualifications as a photojournalist.

Kennerly, a 1972 Pulitzer prize winner for his dramatic combat photographs of the Vietnam war, got his assignment after having spent eight months shadowing then Vice President Gerald Ford for TIME magazine. The job virtually made him part of the family, and when Ford became President his first official act was to name the bearded bachelor as his personal photographer.

Because Kennerly feels he must follow Ford on all his travels abroad, he logged 80,000 miles during the first 10 months of 1975 on Air Force One, the President's private jet plane. On such trips Kennerly is the first to leave Air Force One because that puts him in the best position to get unobstructed head-on shots of the President deplaning. "When he returns to his plane," says Kennerly, "I'm already waiting for him, to get a back shot showing him waving at the crowd."

Wherever Kennerly goes, he is constantly looking for different angles in pursuit of his individualistic view of a "candid presidency." On a state visit to Tokyo, Kennerly boldly walked into the ornate bedroom of the Akasaka Palace to produce the photograph of the President on pages 132-133. Shot with a wide-angle lens, the picture captures the scope of the enormous room, and shows the kind of environment in which the President worked.

This sense of place is a key element in most of the overseas photographs. During Secretary of State Kissinger's summer 1975 round of shuttle diplomacy, which led to Israeli troop withdrawals from the Sinai Desert, Kennerly was the only photographer almost constantly at Kissinger's side. In making the picture of a crucial conference with Egyptian President Anwar Sadat, held out-of-doors near Alexandria *(page 135),* he included the garden and

Backed against an Oval Office wall, White House photographer David Kennerly needed only 10 minutes of the President's time, and afternoon sunlight, to make the official portrait. The result of this informal session hangs in government buildings throughout the United States.

trees in the background, which helped anchor the picture geographically. The same feel for geography also distinguishes the photograph of Kissinger that appears on page 134. Here, Kennerly set his exposure for the glowing city of Jerusalem in the background, and showed the Secretary of State dramatically juxtaposed against it. The photograph contains graphic elements (Kissinger's sharp silhouette, the heavy verticals of the window) that seem to symbolize both the power of the occasion—an imminent accord between Israel and Egypt—and the strength of the man who was instrumental in bringing the agreement about.

In Washington, Kennerly pursues his goal of providing a candid documentation of the Presidency in a highly professional, though sometimes brusque, manner. While covering an Oval Office press conference in September 1975, Kennerly, in a not so subtle choreography of power, moved easily through the jostling mob of journalists, taking pictures of the President from positions around the room denied to others. He moved behind the President's desk to take a shot with a Leica; then from another angle across the room, he used a Nikon with a telephoto lens. In his only nod to propriety, he removed his shoes before he climbed up on a chair to snap away with an odd-looking panoramic camera, a Russian Horizon.

Such behavior may seem excessive. But unlike news photographers, who are assigned to White House news conferences solely to photograph the President, Kennerly was trying to document the meetings in their totality, and from as many different positions as possible. Thus, his Leica was fitted with a wide-angle lens, and was used for photographs of the President chatting with a few newsmen. The Nikon with the telephoto lens was used for close-ups. The Horizon camera is special. It contains a circular housing, inside which lens and shutter rotate to produce a distortion-free photograph showing a range of 140°. With this camera, Kennerly could encompass most of the Oval Office, providing a view not only of the President but also of every one of the newsmen attending the press conference.

Kennerly concedes that his access to the President provided him a "tremendous advantage" over other photographers. Without that advantage, of course, a number of remarkable photographs could not have been taken at all. One such picture is the photograph of Mrs. Ford embracing the President *(page 136),* taken only a short time after the First Lady had returned from the hospital following her operation for breast cancer.

Kennerly's access to high places—and his skill as a photographer—were put to their toughest test during the so-called *Mayaguez* incident. Kennerly was preparing to make a speech on photography in Rochester, New York, when he learned that Cambodian gunboats had seized the unarmed American freighter, *Mayaguez.* Flying back to Washington, he immediately joined

Assignment/**The Presidency**

an emergency meeting of the National Security Council. He was the only nonmember of the Council in the room, but was so unobtrusive that he managed to lug in a 300mm lens and tripod for close-ups of the major participants. Using another telephoto lens, he caught the tense look on the face of Vice President Nelson Rockefeller *(page 128)* while the fate of the *Mayaguez* crew hung in the balance. In 10 nonstop hours, Kennerly shot about 600 pictures, including the climactic moment on pages 128-129 when Ford and Kissinger learned that the *Mayaguez* and its crew had been rescued. By being in the right place at the right time, Kennerly captured, blow by blow, the drama of decision-making at the highest level.

The ability to get such exclusive photographs generated envy, even anger among some of Kennerly's colleagues. Equally irksome to many was Kennerly's unorthodox life style. Unlike his predecessors, who functioned mainly as unobtrusive court historians, the youngest White House photographer in history (he was only 27 when chosen by Ford) stormed the executive mansion in a bold, brash and, said some oldtimers, irreverent manner. Kennerly wore faded jeans and battered desert boots, decorated his office like a battlefield command post with Cambodian flags and signs from Israeli mine fields, and noisily proclaimed himself Washington's swingingest bachelor. "Maybe Kennerly should get his own official photographer," growled one apparently disenchanted newsman.

Kennerly's uninhibited life style resulted in a number of calls for his dismissal during his first year with Ford, demands that a President noted for his loyalty quietly ignored. For his part, Kennerly professed to be undisturbed by such controversy. As the President's chief photographer, he had little time to worry about who was saying what. He supervised a staff of three photographers and a picture editor who, along with Kennerly, were responsible for documenting the Ford Presidency, supplying prints requested by the news media, and shepherding outside photographers on special White House assignments—of which there were more than 40 during 1975.

As the year drew to an end, Kennerly was as busy as ever photographing the President—and trying to keep his feet in the rough and tumble world of White House politics. On the photographic side, at least, he was as confident as ever and as eager to find new angles for his candid pictures. He devised one far-out scheme for a "fly's eye view" of Ford at work, recorded by attaching wide-angle, remote-controlled cameras to the molding around the ceiling of the Oval Office. With this kind of creativity still bubbling, and with the extraordinary collection of photographs he had already made, it was clear that, even if swinger Kennerly should himself become an election-year casualty, he would already have achieved his goal of producing a uniquely intimate look at the Presidency.

Followed by aides, President Ford strides down the checkered hallway of the Executive Office Building after addressing reporters. A 15mm fisheye lens exaggerates the crown-like dome.

Assignment/**The Presidency**

Ramrod-straight Army honor guards with raised umbrellas flank the President as he bids farewell to British Prime Minister Harold Wilson, who was in Washington to discuss international economic problems.

An intent President leans forward to make a point to a visitor aboard Air Force One during a stopover in Chicago. Kennerly shot over the visitor's shoulder to provide a strong foreground, while focusing interest on the President's intent expression.

Assignment/**The Presidency**

The Oval Office rocks with unrestrained jubilation as the President breaks the tension over the Mayaguez crisis—he has received word from Secretary of Defense Schlesinger that the crew of the ship has been freed and is safe.

Tension lines the face of Vice President Nelson Rockefeller as the President briefs the National Security Council on the fate of the Mayaguez, the American vessel captured by Cambodian forces in May 1975. The photograph is one of a series taken during a 10-hour period when top-level meetings were held in the White House on ways to free the ship and its 39-man crew.

Assignment/**The Presidency**

As the President laughed over an old nickname —"Junie"—recalled by Grand Rapids high school chum Silas "Sike" McGee, Kennerly caught Ford and his longtime friend in midchuckle in the East Room of the White House.

Mrs. Ford and daughter, Susan, taking advantage of the President's momentary absence, plop down in tandem in his comfortable Oval Office chair and use his phone to talk with son Michael. This picture was a bonus for Kennerly —taken when the First Lady and her daughter, after a stroll on the White House lawn, walked into the office during a break in a Kennerly-Ford photographic session.

Assignment/**The Presidency**

An enormous, sumptuous bedroom in Tokyo's official guest house for heads of state is the subject of this photograph. But the President, almost overlooked in the background, pursues his work regardless of his surroundings, poring over papers while dressed in the waistcoat, ascot and wing collar he wore—with a tailcoat—for a meeting with the Emperor.

Assignment/**The Presidency**

Silhouetted against the windowed wall of his suite in Jerusalem's King David Hotel, Secretary of State Henry Kissinger waits for a telephone call from President Ford after negotiating an agreement between Egypt and Israel in early September 1975.

In an unusual diplomatic setting—outdoors on the lawn of the villa of Egyptian President Anwar Sadat—Kissinger and the Egyptian leader discuss terms of the Egyptian-Israeli agreement.

Assignment/**The Presidency**

In the family intimacy that is Kennerly's unusual privilege to record, the President gives Mrs. Ford an affectionate hug on her fifth day home from the hospital, where she had undergone surgery for breast cancer.

The New Technology/5

The New Technology/5

Home Holography	140
Color Breakthrough	148
The Sparks of Life	154
Cameras and Equipment	158

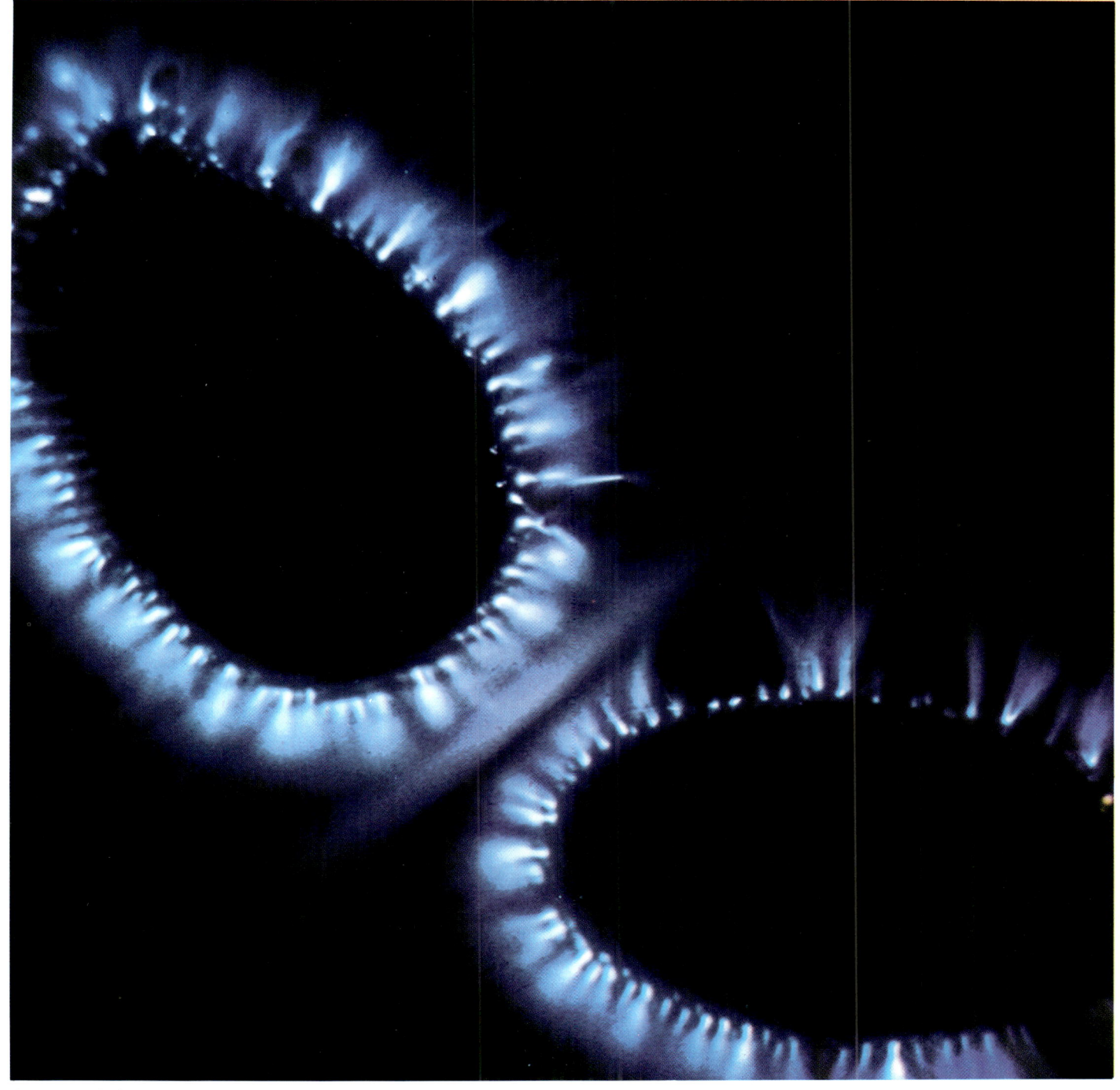

Sparks of Life / THE NEUROPSYCHIATRIC INSTITUTE: *Kirlian Photograph of Subjects' Fingertips during a Simulated Argument,* 1975

The New Technology

Home Holography

Safe, cheap lasers and improved film bring the arcane science of lensless, three-dimensional photography within the reach of the amateur

by Gerald Jonas

> Gerald Jonas, the author of this article, is a staff writer for *The New Yorker* and author of *Visceral Learning*, a study of the conscious control of internal body processes. He is presently working on a book about the brain.

The brightly illuminated image appeared to be hanging in midair in an otherwise darkened room at M. Knoedler & Company, a fashionable New York City art gallery. The subject itself was not special: a diamond necklace dangling from the outstretched fingers of a woman's hand. At a conventional photography show, it would not have been worth a second glance. But this was an exhibit of holograms, strikingly realistic three-dimensional images created by laser light. Like many holograms, the hand and the necklace did not resemble a photographic image at all, but a carving of some shiny material. The illusion of solidity was so convincing that viewers reached out to touch it, only to find themselves passing their hands through thin air.

In the development of holography, 1975 was a watershed year. Two major exhibitions of holograms were staged in New York City, one at Knoedler's and an even larger show at the recently opened International Center for Photography. Both shows attracted large crowds and a great deal of critical comment. But their real importance went beyond mere publicity or prestige; without firsthand experience, no one can appreciate the lifelike quality of a well-made hologram and until these 1975 shows few people outside a laboratory had ever seen a hologram. Even fewer were aware that, thanks to recent advances in equipment, virtually anyone can now put together a holographic darkroom and begin making holograms on his own.

Like any photograph, the hologram starts with the exposure of a light-sensitive emulsion to light reflected off an object. The emulsion most often used is the familiar one, a thin film of silver-halide crystals applied to a sheet of plastic or a glass plate. But there the resemblance ends. Unlike a photograph, a hologram contains no recognizable image; it is like a phonograph record that must be played back before its contents are revealed. To play back a hologram, the film must be illuminated by a bright beam of light. When this is done properly, the image of the recorded object suddenly appears, not on the surface of the film but suspended in air somewhere in front or in back of it: the hologram captures on film all the visual information the human eye needs to see objects in three dimensions.

The amateur photographer who wants to try his hand at holography can find all the help he needs in the lively do-it-yourself movement that has sprung up around this new medium. Special equipment required for a holographic darkroom can be ordered through a number of mail-order supply houses. Many colleges now have holography courses and there are schools in San Francisco and New York City devoted exclusively to teaching holography. Both Kodak and AGFA manufacture special film and plates—coated with a very fine-grain emulsion—for use in holography; an even faster holographic film, Kodak's SO-253, now increases the novice's chances of making good holograms under less-than-ideal conditions. Unquestionably, however, the single most important piece of equipment that a holographer needs is a laser. Until now, lasers have been complicated, costly and dangerous devices; but in the last few years small and relatively inexpensive lasers—$175 and up —have become available, although they must still be used with caution.

One type of laser often used in holography resembles a fat rifle barrel that shoots light of a very special kind. Its barrel seals in a mixture of neon and helium gases that glow like those in a neon sign when an electric current is passed through them. But in a laser, the gases give a pencil-thin beam of intensely red light, quite different from that emitted by a sign.

Laser light performs a special role in the holographic process because it turns to picture-making advantage certain aspects of the wavelike structure of light. All light can be thought of as waves of energy that oscillate between high points and low points, somewhat like the crests and troughs of a series of ocean waves. The distance from one crest to the next, called the wavelength, determines color. Most familiar light sources, such as the sun or an electric bulb, emit a jumble of light waves of many different lengths. This jumble makes "white" light; when such light is filtered so that only a narrow range of wavelengths reaches the eye, it is perceived as a single color, such as the red glow of a darkroom bulb. But even if the filter could pass only a single wavelength (an impossible dream), the light would still be partially jumbled—"incoherent"—because the individual waves would not necessarily oscillate in step with each other. In truly coherent light the distance from crest to crest is exactly the same in every wave, and the waves rise and fall in perfect unison, like a well-disciplined marching band. The only light that even approaches this ideal of coherence is the light produced by a laser.

Laser light is much purer in color than other light because its waves are almost all of one length. But even more important for holographic purposes is the rigid discipline of these waves. If two beams of incoherent light (say, from flashlights) cross each other, the result is merely more incoherent light: a jumble plus a jumble makes more jumble. When two laser beams cross, they do not produce a jumble at all, but combine to form an entirely new wave pattern. The crests and troughs add in some places and cancel one another out in others, creating a new wave structure that is called an interference pattern; a hologram is a film record of such an interference pattern.

The first step in making a hologram is to take a single beam of laser light and split it into two beams. (A complete home darkroom holography setup is illustrated on pages 144-145.) Splitting the beam requires a semitransparent mirror near the business end of the laser. Some of the emerging light is reflected from the silvery surface of the mirror; the rest passes straight through. This leaves two beams of coherent laser light traveling separate paths, but since both beams have a common target—a sheet of unexposed film clamped

The New Technology / **Home Holography**

in a holder a few feet from the laser—each beam must be guided toward the film by mirrors, lenses, prisms and other optical devices. One beam (known as the reference beam) is allowed to reach the film without undergoing change; it arrives with all its waves still in lock step. But the second beam (known as the object beam) is detoured so that, before striking the film, it bounces off the subject of the picture. After colliding with the subject the light waves rebound at various angles. The wave forms are altered but the beam retains its lock-step coherence with the reference beam.

The light scattered by the object and the light of the reference beam meet again on the film. Because both are still coherent, they combine on the film to form an interference pattern. But the reflected beam has changed slightly. The changes, which bear the distinctive "mark" of the object, are preserved in the interference pattern. In some places, a wave of light from the reference beam and a wave of light from the object beam reinforce each other, causing the light to become brighter, strongly exposing the film. In other places, the two light waves cancel out, and the film records nothing at all. The result is a pattern of bands of exposed and unexposed film.

When holographic film is developed—like an ordinary negative—the actual interference pattern cannot be seen with the naked eye because the dark and light bands are much too fine; there may be as many as 20,000 bands per square inch. Viewed under a microscope, the pattern resembles the elaborate whorls and swirls of a fingerprint. But the viewer has no way of knowing what image these shapes represent until the final, and most dramatic, step in the process: reconstructing the three-dimensional image by shining a bright light at the film. To bring the image to life, the reconstruction beam must strike the film at the same angle that the reference beam made during the recording. At this angle, the dark and light bands of the interference pattern bend and block and redirect the light waves of the reconstruction beam to create a virtual replica of the light originally scattered by the object. This set of light waves is what reaches the viewer. The reconstructed holographic image looks real because it is identical to what the eye would see if it were viewing the original object illuminated by laser light.

Making a hologram is not as difficult as it sounds, although it does demand painstaking attention to detail. The basic problem is stability. The all-important dark and light bands are so thin and so close together that if the object or the film or either of the two beams moves so much as a millionth of an inch during exposure, the pattern will be smeared. If it is, the result is not blurring but total destruction of the picture—no image can be reconstructed. So the prerequisite to holography is a means of keeping the equipment motionless during the exposure. This problem is further complicated by the fact that home darkroom holography requires long exposures. There are two rea-

SELWYN LISSACK: *Hologram of Sam Rivers*, 1974

Floating inside a transparent drum, a three-dimensional image of a jazz musician moves clockwise (from upper left) as the drum revolves. Such a 360° hologram not only reveals all sides of an object but also depicts motion.

sons: the small helium-neon laser most appropriate for home use puts out very little power; and holographic film must be extremely fine-grained (therefore very slow) in order to record an interference pattern at all. Exposure times vary with conditions, and usually must be determined by trial and error; but the beginning holographer should be prepared to maintain a stable work surface in his darkroom for a minimum of 10 seconds.

In a sense, the holographer's darkroom *is* his camera. He not only develops film there; he sets up his lights, subject and film, and records his image there as well. Many beginners build their holographic darkroom in a basement with a concrete floor. They make a large, deep, rectangular well of concrete blocks and fill the center with clean sand. The laser is secured to one side of the concrete well; the optical components—beam-splitter, mirrors to guide the laser beams, film-holder, object-holder—are firmly attached to metal or plastic stakes, which are driven into the sand where needed. Finally, the subject to be recorded—a small object like a toy locomotive or pair of bronzed baby shoes—is placed in front of the film-holder.

The basic split-beam arrangement, which most holographers start with, produces what is known as a transmission hologram. During the recording stage, the reference beam and the object beam both strike the film from the same side, although at slightly different angles. This kind of hologram can be reconstructed with another laser beam, or even an ordinary flashlight beam with a red or yellow filter. Once the holographer has mastered the transmission hologram, he can go on to achieve variations by rearranging the optical components that guide the laser beams to the film. For example, if the emulsion is mounted on transparent material (like a glass plate) and the reference and object beams are allowed to converge on it from opposite sides, a reflection hologram is created. This kind of hologram can be hung on a wall and reconstructed by the light from an ordinary bulb; in fact, it looks almost like a conventional print—except that the image it projects has the three-dimensional quality of a transmission hologram.

Further refinements include holograms in color, and second-generation holograms, which start with reconstructed holographic images instead of actual objects. Making holograms out of holograms requires great skill, but the results can be spectacular: the eerie apparition of the hand and necklace that was the hit of the show at Knoedler's was created in a multistep process, beginning with a hologram recorded in the light from a ruby laser.

The future of holography is still very much up in the air. Until now, its development has been largely in the hands of scientists and engineers. But if the early history of photography is any guide, the main impetus to realizing its full potential may come from the ranks of amateur experimenters—who approach it not as a curiosity but as a new medium of self-expression.

The New Technology/**Home Holography**

A Laser in the Basement

Using readily available materials, the amateur photographer can produce holograms at home. The optical setup on the opposite page—arranged to make a transmission hologram—fully meets standards of stability and flexibility needed to make high quality holograms. The essential components on the table are shown in detail at right.

The best place in the house to work is the basement, where a concrete floor helps insulate the equipment from outside vibrations. The workshop area should also be free from rapid fluctuations in temperature and humidity.

The first step in producing a basement hologram is to construct the optical table—in this case with a concrete base and walls of concrete blocks. Sand is used to stabilize the table and to anchor its optical components—one of which is a beam splitter that divides the laser's light into the two beams of unequal intensity that are necessary to produce a hologram. To place these components correctly, turn on the laser and move them about until the laser's split beams take paths to the film that are similar to those shown in the drawing.

Next, turn off the lights and take a meter reading from the film position. Then, with the film in the film holder, test expose with laser light so that the meter can be calibrated for future sessions. Once exposed, film is developed normally and is then ready to view.

A rotating mirror is the first component met by the laser beam. The mirror assembly is made by gluing a flat mirror to a piece of plastic, rounded and shaped as shown, that fits into a plastic pipe. The pipe, in turn, is attached to the table wall, and the mirror fitted into the top of the pipe with enough play so it can be turned by hand. Like others in the setup, this mirror has a silver coating on its front surface.

Either convex or concave lenses, like those in powerful eyeglasses, may be used to spread the beams sufficiently to illuminate the film. Here a lens has been glued over a hole cut in a plastic sheet, which in turn is glued into a slotted plastic tube. The shorter the focal length of the lens, the greater the beam's divergence.

A piece of ground glass serves as the diffuser; sometimes it is used with a lens in front of it to increase the spread of the beam and further soften the harshness of the highly directional laser light. The diffuser is attached to a slotted tube of its own and staked into the sand in the same manner as the beam splitter.

The basic beam splitter is a second type of mirror, which allows part of the laser light directed at it to pass through while reflecting the rest. The beam splitter is mounted by gluing it into the slotted end of a plastic tube, which has been tapered on the other end so that it can be staked into the sand of the optical table.

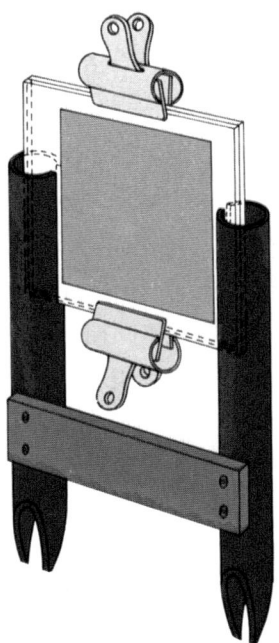

The film is held between two sheets of glass clamped by strong spring clips. Long slots in two plastic tubes receive the film holder, and allow film to be slipped into place after preliminary positioning and exposure measurements have been made. If a sensitized glass plate (more rigid but far more costly than film) is used instead of film, the plate can be placed directly into similar slotted tubes.

A Pitcher in Space

The homemade table at right shows components arranged to make a hologram of a pitcher. To start the laser beam, switch on the power supply. The beam first passes the shutter, a cardboard flag that can be raised and lowered without disturbing the work area. A mirror directs the beam to the beam splitter, which reflects a portion of the beam while allowing about 90 per cent to pass through. The transmitted portion is called the object beam (dark gray); the reflected portion is the reference beam (light gray).

The object beam strikes the mirror in the right corner of the table, and ricochets toward the pitcher through a diffuser which spreads the beam. The light is then reflected onto the film. A baffle prevents object-beam light from hitting the film before striking the pitcher.

Meanwhile the reference beam is deflected by a mirror on the left side of the table, then passes through a lens which spreads it to cover the film. A sensitive exposure meter calculates exposure and verifies that the reference beam is about four times brighter than the object beam (now reduced in intensity by diffusion and reflection). A second baffle blocks light scattered from the beam splitter. When the hologram is viewed, by shining laser light through it, a three-dimensional image of the pitcher appears.

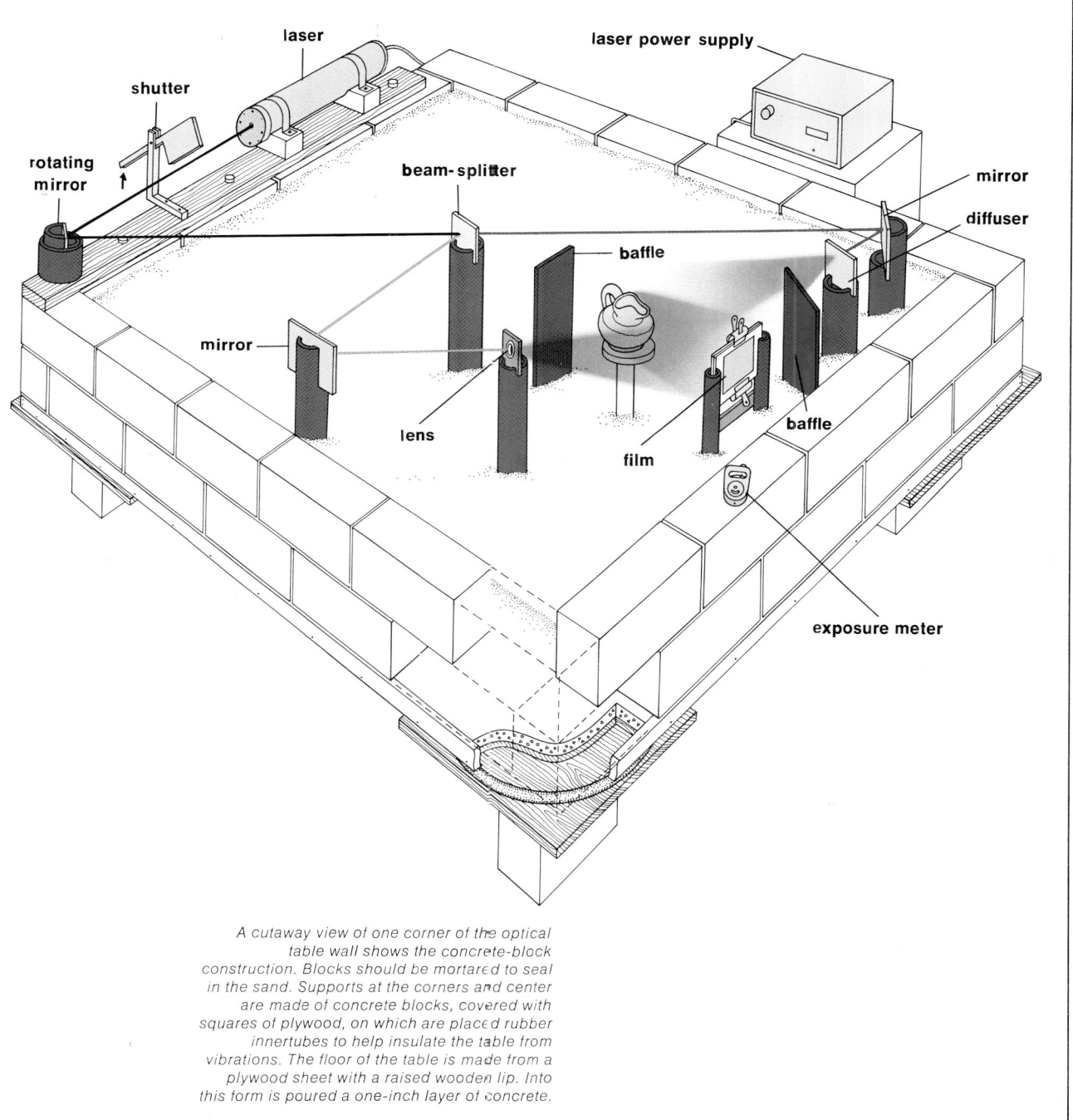

A cutaway view of one corner of the optical table wall shows the concrete-block construction. Blocks should be mortared to seal in the sand. Supports at the corners and center are made of concrete blocks, covered with squares of plywood, on which are placed rubber innertubes to help insulate the table from vibrations. The floor of the table is made from a plywood sheet with a raised wooden lip. Into this form is poured a one-inch layer of concrete.

The New Technology/**Home Holography**

Dali in 3-D

Holography moved out of the laboratory in 1975 and into the art world when Surrealism's *ancien terrible,* Salvador Dali, joined other artists for a series of New York City holography exhibits.

Not unexpectedly, Dali's works were the most audacious and visually pleasing examples of a fledgling form that has been notable for its awkward esthetics. Indeed, holography seems a natural progression for Dali, a Surrealist artist whose paintings often give an uncanny illusion of depth. Two of his works are shown on these pages, along with an explanation of how one of them was accomplished.

The hologram, *Dali Painting Gala,* is a three-dimensional image of the artist painting his wife. The entire scene floats in a transparent plastic drum, topped by a frieze of vermeil and silver. As the drum turns, the figures inside rotate like Lilliputians trapped in a cage.

The most ambitious of all Dali's holograms, *Holos, Holos, Gabor!* (a title referring to holography's inventor, Dennis Gabor) shows hardhats playing cards, while behind and through them loom parts of Velázquez's famous painting, *Las Meninas*. The work was executed to Dali's specifications by New York holographer Selwyn Lissack. Holograms were made of each scene and then combined to form the world's first holographic collage.

Dali's mockup for Holos, Holos, Gabor! contains, on separate panels, parts of Velázquez's painting, Las Meninas, including a self-portrait of Velázquez himself. The finished hologram (below, right) is based on the multipanel mockup and also contains a scene of beer drinkers playing cards.

◄ Master illusionist Salvador Dali poses next to a hologram of himself and his wife reflected in two mirrors. The halo-like spot over Dali's head—a surrealist flourish —was purposely caused by reflecting the camera's flash in the mirror behind him.

Dali's completed Velázquez-inspired hologram glows in ghostly depth as light illuminates the card players, the face of Velázquez and the rearranged parts of Las Meninas. Dali's work appeared in an exhibition in New York City.

The New Technology

Breakthrough in Color Prints

A refinement of the silver dye-bleach process allows the nonprofessional to produce sharp, fade-resistant prints from slides

Amateur photographers who have despaired of making prints from color slides in their own darkrooms got good news in 1975. A long-established commercial process for producing sharp, brilliant, fade-resistant prints was perfected for home use. Known as Cibachrome, and based on a principle called silver dye-bleaching, the new process differs in one vital way from the most frequently used home printing methods.

Normally, silver compounds in the emulsion guide the chemical formation of color dyes. With Cibachrome, however, the color dyes are already present and, in this system, the silver guides the bleaching-out of proportions of some of the dyes. The remaining colors form the final print—and if current research can be brought to fruition, this same system may someday be made to generate original color slides as well.

The results of the new home printing process can be dramatic: finely detailed long-lasting prints with richly colored dyes, and an overall impression of quality previously associated with custom lab work. Moreover, the procedures are simple; processing time is short; the usual stringent temperature controls are unnecessary. As a consequence, even a beginner can turn out excellent color prints.

The theory of producing color images by bleaching out dyes was first advanced at the turn of the century, but at that time no one could combine dyes and bleaches effectively nor apply the emulsion layers to the required thinness and uniformity. The breakthrough was made in the late 1920s by Bela Gaspar, a student of medicine and chemistry, and one of many researchers then pursuing a practical process for recording photographic images in color. By 1930 Gaspar had moved to Germany and was devoting himself full time to color photographic research. In 1933, he exhibited the first color movie based on the silver dye-bleach process. Though imperfect, this movie print, which he called Gasparcolor, contained emulsion layers that were relatively thin and uniform.

Over the next decade, Gaspar—fleeing Nazism first to Belgium and then, in 1940, to the United States—improved his process so that he could reproduce more closely the subtle colorings of real life. During World War II, he applied Gasparcolor to still prints, working with the United States Army to make copies of color photographs for engineering research. Many of these prints survive today with their colors largely unchanged by time.

Though technically successful and widely renowned among scientists for his research, Gaspar was a poor businessman. Over the years he collaborated with many different manufacturers, but he refused to be tied to any of them. As a result, he never reaped much commercial benefit from his silver dye-bleach system, although it had, indeed, established the groundwork for a product that was marketable on a large scale.

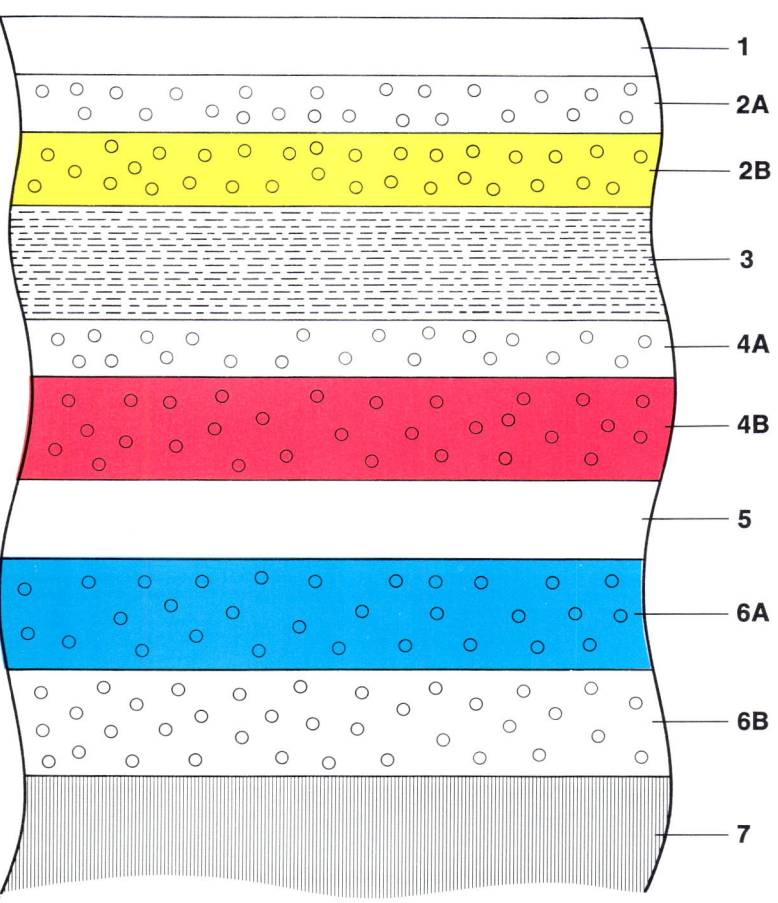

Cibachrome emulsion is built up in nine layers (including three layer-pairs), each responding to a third of the light spectrum. The top layer (1) is a protective gelatin. The first pair (2A and 2B) responds to blue light, with silver compounds (white disks) in both layers, and yellow dye only in layer 2B. Below this is a separating layer of gelatin (3). The second layer-pair, which responds to green light, has silver compounds (4A) and a combination of silver compounds and magenta dye (4B). Another layer of gelatin (5) follows. The third pair (6A and 6B) responds to red light. The cyan dye and silver compound layer (6A) is on top, to keep all dye layers close together and reduce image blurring. The layers rest on a base of white plastic (7).

The giant step into the marketplace was taken in 1963 by the Swiss chemical company, Ciba, Ltd., which evolved and marketed—but for professional laboratories only—a process called Cibachrome based on Gaspar's work. It is a simplification of this custom lab system that became available to the home printmaker in 1975.

With the new Cibachrome process, a slide is first placed in the enlarger and projected onto the print material. Once exposed, Cibachrome needs only three chemical baths, whereas other common systems need at least five. The first bath, the developer, turns exposed light-sensitive silver compounds into metallic silver. The second bath, a bleach, reacts with the metallic silver and destroys nearby dyes. The last bath dissolves the silver compounds, leaving behind dye molecules that display a positive image of the original slide. Both the process and resulting print demonstrate several other major advantages over prior systems:

- Cibachrome processing is tolerant of a considerable range in temperature. In normal home printmaking processes the average temperature can vary only 1 to 2°F. from that recommended—usually 100°F. But with Cibachrome all processing stages can be performed in 12 minutes at room temperature (between 72°F. and 78°F. One chemical-mixing step, however, requires hot water of approximately 100°F.). Processing steps will also work successfully at temperatures as low as 65° and as high as 85°—if the processing time is correspondingly lengthened or shortened.
- A Cibachrome print is highly resistant to destruction by light. The three dyes present in the emulsion—cyan, magenta and yellow—are hardy ones known as azo dyes. All dyes fade over the years, but these azo dyes fade slowly and at a uniform rate. Although a Cibachrome print image steadily weakens over the years if not stored in darkness, it does not, for example, turn the ghastly green that characterizes some prints.
- A Cibachrome print is sharp. In all home processes, including Cibachrome, some light used during the initial exposing step is absorbed by the silver compounds, and some is scattered. This tends to diffuse the image. However, Cibachrome dyes absorb almost all of this scattered light and in this way the image-blur is reduced.

Ironically it is this last advantage as a printing process that presently handicaps Cibachrome as a camera film to produce color slides. The absorption so necessary for sharp prints reduces scattering of light within the emulsion, but scattered light makes an emulsion more sensitive because it exposes more of the emulsion's silver compounds. Until a way is found to increase its sensitivity without a loss in print sharpness, Cibachrome features will not be available in a camera film—but it will continue to be a great boon to home printmakers.

The New Technology/**Color Breakthrough**

The Chemistry of Cibachrome

To turn a slide of four differently colored balls on a green pool table *(near right)* into a finished print *(far right)*, the print material must go through the stages shown here.

First, it must be exposed *(enlarger symbol)*, and then processed through three chemical baths *(drum symbols)*. What happens within the material at each of the stages is shown in the schematic diagrams above each symbol. In these diagrams, Cibachrome's nine-layered emulsion structure is simplified into three vertical stripes, each corresponding to one of the three types of light-sensitive layers in the emulsion. The trios of separated images above the second and fourth stages indicate the appearance of each of the layers at that point in the printing process.

After processing, the material is washed and dried—and the Cibachrome print is ready to view. When illuminated for viewing, dyes remaining in the print absorb light from different parts of the color spectrum in different degrees.

For example, the white cue ball in the slide becomes a white ball in the print because all the obstructing dyes are removed in that area and all light is reflected back to the viewer; the green cloth appears green because green-absorbing magenta dye has been bleached away, and green light reflects back. In this way each of the slide's colors will be reproduced in the final print.

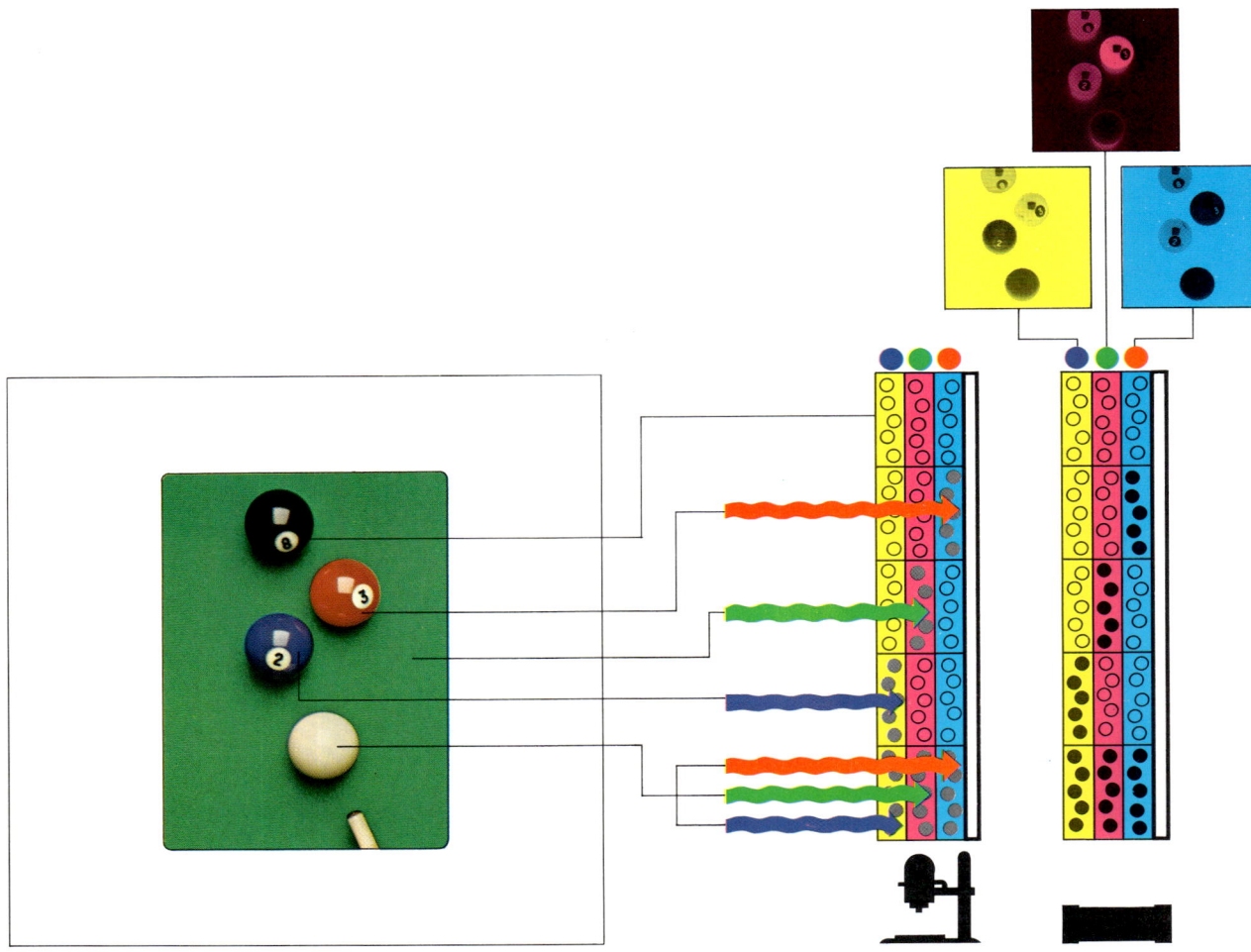

In printmaking the projecting light takes on colors as it passes through the color slide; as the colors strike the print material they affect different layers in its emulsion. The black eight ball blocks all colors and thus does not affect the print material at all (see line from ball to diagram). The red ball transmits light to the red-sensitive (cyan-dyed) layer; the green pool table transmits light to the green-sensitive (magenta-dyed) layer, and so on. The white ball transmits all colors and thus affects all layers. Silver compounds exposed by the enlarging light are represented by gray disks; white disks represent unexposed compounds. In the developing bath (above right), exposed silver compounds are converted into metallic silver (black disks) that will control the bleaching of dyes.

During the bleach bath, dye-bleach molecules diffuse through the emulsion layers. When they contact metallic silver (black disks), they react with them and are then ready in their changed state to bleach the dye. The bleach molecules do this by continuing their random migration until they encounter nearby dye molecules, which they then break up. As the dyes are destroyed, another, slower reaction converts the metallic silver back to a compound so that it can be dissolved in the fixer. Both processes continue until all the metallic silver is returned to compound form.

The fixing bath dissolves the silver compounds, and a wash step then follows to remove the broken dye molecules and chemical residues. All that remains is the unaffected dye that reproduces the colors of the original slide. When the processed print (right, above) is viewed, the magenta-dye pattern (top) absorbs proportions of green from the white light used for viewing. Red and blue are reflected to the eye. Similarly, the yellow-dye pattern absorbs proportions of blue light, allowing red and green to be reflected to the eye. The cyan-dye pattern absorbs red light, letting blue and green reach the eye. The sum total of these effects is a sharp, full-color image.

The New Technology/**Color Breakthrough**

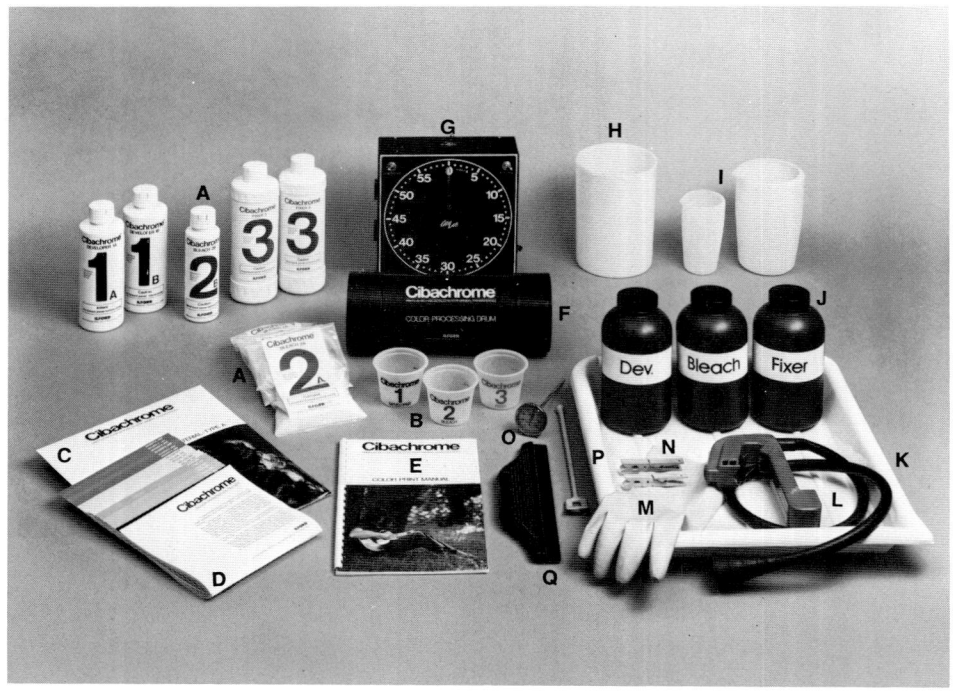

A	processing chemicals	
B	measuring cups	
C	print material	
D	filters	
E	manual	
F	processing drum	
G	timer	
H	half-gallon container	
I	graduates	
J	solution storage bottles	
K	washing tray	
L	washing siphon	
M	gloves	
N	clothes pins	
O	thermometer	
P	stirring rod	
Q	squeegee	

Making a Cibachrome Print

Materials needed to produce Cibachrome prints are shown above. The items on the left side of the illustration are supplied especially by Cibachrome's manufacturer. These include a chemical kit with measuring cups (A and B); color-print material (C); and a book of instructions (E). The Cibachrome people also provide: plastic color-printing filters (D) and a light-tight processing drum (F) for photographers who may not already own them. The filters, 6 inches square, are needed in enlarging and can be cut by home developers to fit their equipment. The drum is more convenient than trays for processing prints, since it can be handled with the lights on.

The remaining darkroom materials (G to Q) on the right hand side of the picture are standard for home processing. The proper procedures for using these materials to produce a print are shown at right.

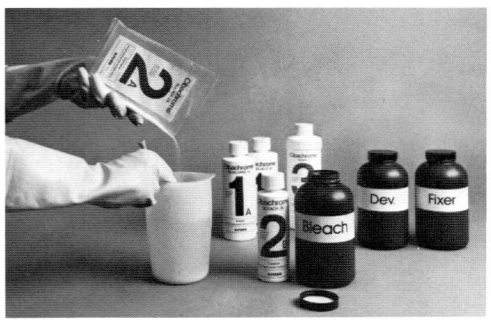

1 | *Begin by preparing the solutions, which are easily mixed. Only Part 2A of the bleach is a powder. Pour a little of this powder at a time into 100° F. water, stirring until it dissolves.*

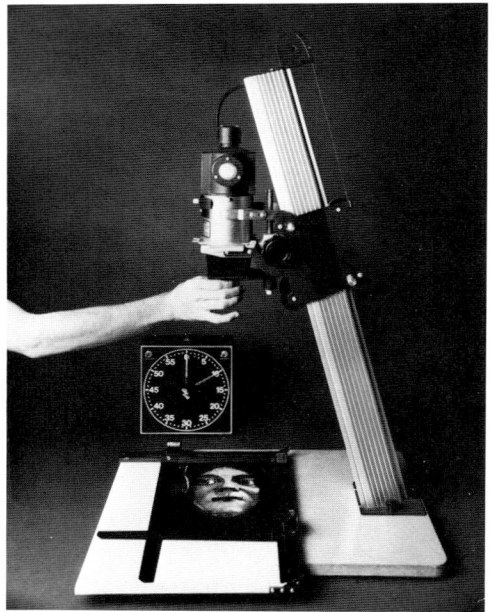

2 | *Place a transparency in the enlarger. Turn off the lights, switch on the enlarger and expose the slide. As in normal darkroom practice, the first print should be a test, to determine what exposure and set of filters are required for an accurate final print. Because making a print directly from a slide is a positive-to-positive process (unlike printing from a negative), greater exposure will make the print lighter; heavier filtration will add more of a filter's color to the print. All the following steps apply to both the test and the finished prints.*

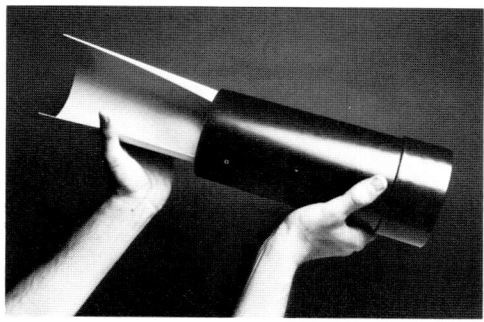

3 | Curl the print toward the emulsion and put it into a dry, clean drum. Seal the drum. Turn on the lights. If trays are used, keep the lights off until ready for the fixing stage.

4 | Measure out each solution—developer (1), bleach (2) and fixer (3)—to the amount shown on the measuring card. Follow the sequence of steps 5,6,7 three times, once for each solution.

5 | Set the timer for each stage and pour the solutions from cup to processing drum. At room temperature—between 72° and 78° F. Total processing time will be 12 minutes.

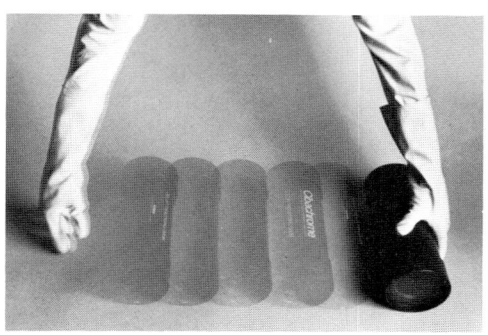

6 | To prevent streaking caused by uneven spread of the solutions, agitate the processing drum smoothly back and forth by rolling it on the top of your darkroom table.

7 | Drain each solution after use. Developer is drained after 1¾ minutes; bleach after 3¾ minutes; fixer after 3 minutes. Store bleach in a separate half-gallon container for neutralizing.

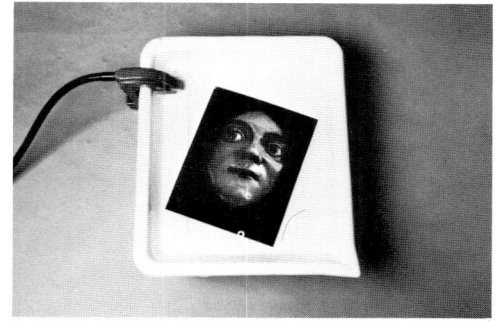

8 | Carefully remove the print from the drum and wash it in rapidly flowing water. However, do not let the stream of water strike the print directly because it could damage the surface.

9 | Drop two neutralizer tablets into the half-gallon container of bleach. The tablets will dissolve with a fizz. When the fizzing stops, the bleach can be safely drained.

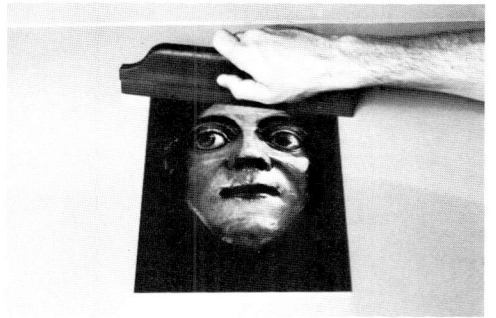

10 | To hasten drying, squeegee the print gently. Never use a hot drum drier: Cibachrome has a plastic base, and water trapped between the base and the drum can prevent drying.

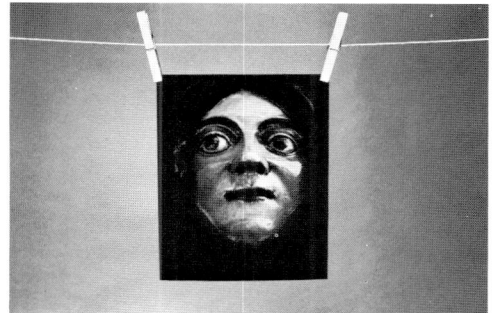

11 | For final drying, the print may be placed on an absorbent surface or hung up (as shown). For extra speed, use a warm-air blower, which will produce a dry print in a few minutes.

The New Technology

The Sparks of Life

Experiments in Kirlian photography are enabling scientists to fix and study the fields of energy that radiate from living things

Imagine this: at a party someone claims to see colored halos or auras radiating from everyone around him. He says the rays of color shimmer in various hues, change from bright to dim, lengthen or shorten, and that from these changes he can tell who is happy, who is angry, who is about to be ill. Until recently, almost anyone but a mystic listening in on the conversation would have dismissed the talker as some kind of fool. And, indeed, science is convinced that nobody can actually see such radiation with the naked eye. But thanks to a startling kind of photograph, named after its Russian originators, Semyon and Valentina Kirlian, such auras actually have been recorded on film —and it is possible that they may even provide accurate gauges of physical and mental health.

Kirlian photographs are made in a darkened room without a camera or lens. A photographic subject, a coin, say, or a person's finger, is wired to one electrode and an unexposed sheet of film is placed in contact with a second electrode. The subject is touched to the emulsion surface of the film and the current is turned on. The electrical discharge exposes silver-halide crystals in the emulsion, and a latent image of the object—and its mysterious aura —is recorded. The picture is then developed in the normal way.

Inanimate objects that have been photographed by the Kirlian apparatus produce steady, fixed auras. But animate objects give off auras that vary enormously. For example, if a man and a woman who love each other put their hands close together, their auras may be connected, although the hands are not actually touching. If the man and woman quarrel, their auras can separate. Even more fascinating is the so-called Creeping Charley phenomenon. This occurs when a common leaf—in one of the pilot American experiments a leaf from a ground-creeping plant called a Creeping Charley—has a piece chopped from it and a Kirlian photograph is made of the remainder. A ghostly image of the *entire leaf* appears *(opposite)*.

The implications of the auras are enormous, but the real meaning has long perplexed scientists. For years the business of unraveling the mystery was not helped by the fact that researchers in Russia and the United States, the two countries most interested in Kirlian techniques, had been making photographs with instruments of widely varied design—with equally varied results. However, a major step toward remedying the situation was taken in 1975, when physicists, biologists, physicians and electrical technicians at the New Jersey Institute of Technology established a unique new think tank called International Kirlian Research Associates. The New Jersey investigators are busy gathering and disseminating data that will allow them to design improved apparatus of their own in an effort to put Kirlian researchers around the globe on the same wave length. Once these efforts are coordinated, and standardized equipment and criteria established, the association

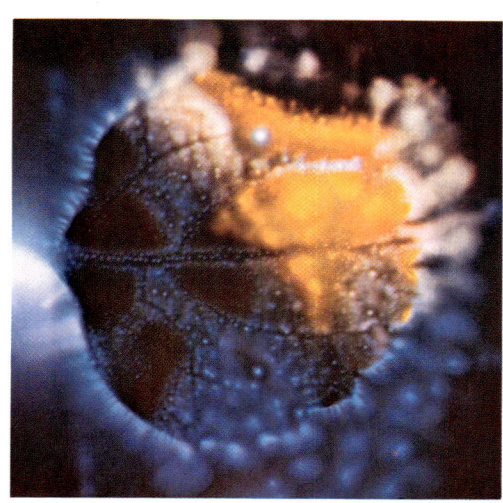

The dazzling coronae that dance around in Kirlian photographs like this one of a damaged leaf have mystified scientists around the world. Part of the leaf has been torn away; yet when an electrical charge is applied to the remaining piece (dark brown), pinpricks of light fill in the leaf's entire original shape, with the excised section showing up as a ghostly gold and white.

believes science will be within reach of an understanding of what the auras really mean—and perhaps how knowledge of them can be practically applied in psychiatry and physical medicine.

This goal is a long way removed from the primitive discovery of Kirlian photography almost 40 years ago in Russia. While working in 1939 as an electrician in Kranscdar, a city by the Black Sea, Semyon Kirlian was watching a hospital demonstration of a high-frequency physiotherapy machine. Noticing a spark jump the small gap between the electrode and the patient's skin, he wondered how the spark would show up on a photographic plate. To find out, he attached electrodes to one of his fingers, pressed it onto a sheet of film, threw a switch—and gave himself a severe burn. But that painful experience paid off. Upon processing the film, Kirlian was startled to see the image of his finger fringed with a fuzzy aura.

Fascinated, Kirlian and his wife Valentina set about making more of the bizarre photographs, using a relatively harmless alternating-current oscillator, rather than shock-inducing direct current, to generate up to 200,000 sparks per second. They then proceeded to hook Kirlian apparatus to numerous objects—some of which produced auras that were startlingly different with each experimental exposure.

News of their work spread quickly among sympathetic Soviet scientists, but support from the government took much longer. In a land dedicated to hardheaded and pragmatic progress, anyone photographing inexplicable halos seemed to be dabbling in the useless—and thus forbidden—area of mysticism. Finally in the late 1960s, 20 years after their first experiments, several eminent Soviet scientists vouched for the scientific merits of their work and the Kirlians began to receive government support in the form of a well-equipped laboratory and research funds.

If the Kirlians were finally accepted by the Soviet government, their work was still greeted unenthusiastically by much of the scientific community. Most of the controversy centered around experimental findings with animate objects. For example, the Kirlians reported that a freshly plucked leaf displayed a dazzling aura and that a few hours later, when the leaf died, its aura faded. Kirlian also said that when he was tense or tired his own auras were radically different than when he was in a relaxed mood. And once when he was ill, he noted that the auras around his hands "showed a chaotic, blurred and cloudy pattern." By contrast, a healthy Valentina's hands showed auras that were sharp and brightly colored. Their conclusion: the auras somehow reflected varying states of health.

Their followers agreed. But at least one critic, a leading biophysicist, stated flatly that auras produced by any object were nothing more than "the cold emission of electrons" energized by the electrical field applied to the object

The New Technology/**Sparks of Life**

under study. Other anti-Kirlians also maintained—with some justification —that the experiments themselves contained too many variables, such as current frequency and type of film and temperature, that could change the color and shape of auras. Furthermore, they pointed out, each object that undergoes Kirlian photography creates its special problems: a leaf may produce its own micro-climate of moisture and electrical resistance that in turn may cause changes in the recorded auras. In a fingertip, the skin's humidity, electrical resistance, and chemical content all change from second to second. Finally, experimental apparatus itself affects the object to be photographed.

However, Kirlian advocates have one piece of evidence that defies all the theories: the photographs in which a severed leaf seems to remember its missing half when exposed to Kirlian apparatus. The first experiment involving this sort of Kirlian effect was performed in 1968 by Soviet researchers at Kazakh State University in Alma-Ata. The resulting photograph of a severed leaf showing the leaf's full outline was, they claimed, an indication that all living things possess a so-called counterpart body that is a loose blueprint of the original physical object.

In the United States, a U.C.L.A. clinical psychologist named Thelma Moss was fascinated by reports of the work at Alma-Ata. In 1970, she went to see for herself how the Russian experiments were performed, but the Soviet government thwarted her efforts by refusing her access to Kirlian laboratories. Therefore, the Moss team had to reconstruct experiments, and design equipment of their own—which, in hundreds of tests, failed to produce the desired results. Then in 1973 they built a machine that produced a picture of the missing part of a severed leaf taken from a Creeping Charley plant.

Since 1973 the Moss team has devised some other fascinating experiments. One of the most unusual was conducted in 1975 when the scientists asked paired volunteers to put their fingertips on a Kirlian apparatus and imagine feelings of intense affection or hostility. The resulting pictures *(at left, opposite, top to bottom)* showed barriers of a pale color between the fingers of couples who simulated an argument. When the couples imagined sexual attraction, however, a red blur connected their auras. And when a real argument actually broke out between two volunteers, one subject's aura turned brilliant red while the other's was extinguished.

The possible practical applications of these findings are limitlessly intriguing. For example, auras could some day be used by psychiatrists as early warning signals of depression or emotional instability in patients. And if scientists are able to pinpoint exactly which auras are indicative of hard-to-trace diseases like cancer and leukemia, the auras could be used to spot these killing maladies at their inception, giving physicians a better chance to save human lives.

Changes of color and image in three Kirlian photographs of the finger tips of a man and a woman are interpreted as indicating mood changes. Blue halos are divided by a bar during a simulated argument (top). After a request to fantasize sexual attraction (center), the images blurred red. In a real argument (bottom), the woman's aura is extinguished.

The Kirlian images of a volunteer subject's finger are attributed to the accumulated effects of alcohol. Before imbibing (top), the aura consisted of a semicircle of constrained dots. After the man downed 17 ounces of liquor at 15-minute intervals (bottom), the aura of his finger tip had rounded out into a brilliant blob outlined against his skin markings.

Marijuana appears to cause aura changes comparable to those exhibited in the alcohol experiment. The finger tips of two volunteers who had not yet begun to smoke (top) gave off separate, crescent-shaped coronas. But after the subjects smoked a marijuana cigarette (bottom), their auras joined in glowing harmony—perhaps a reflection of their shared euphoria.

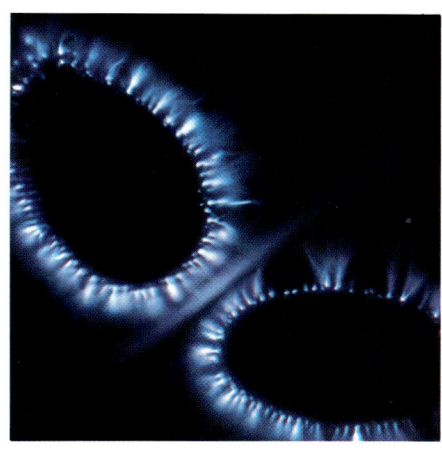
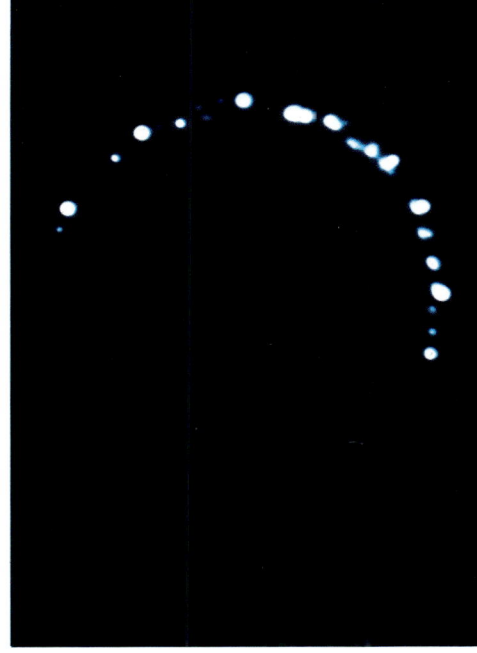
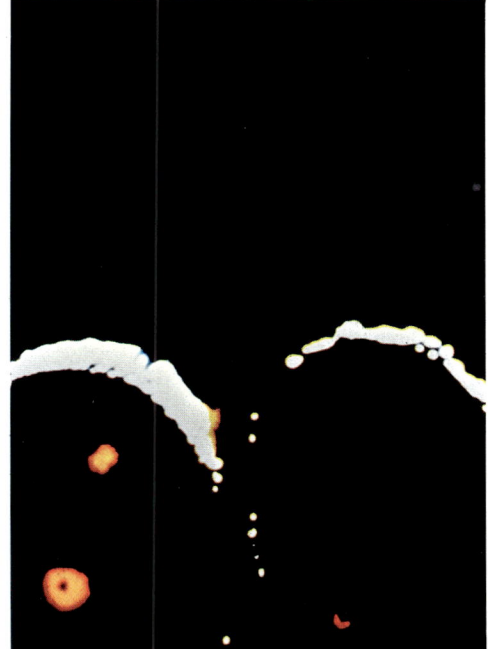
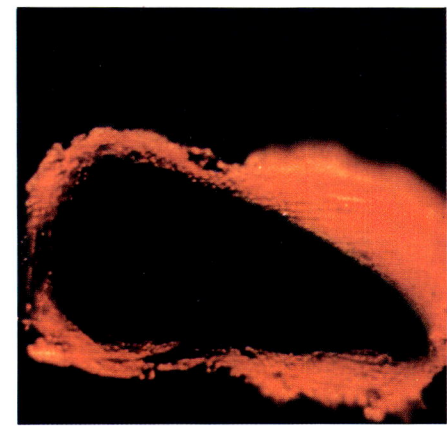
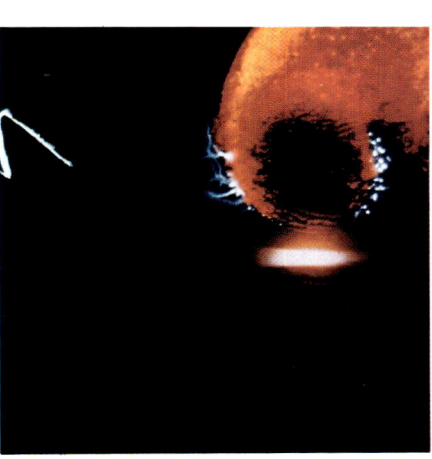
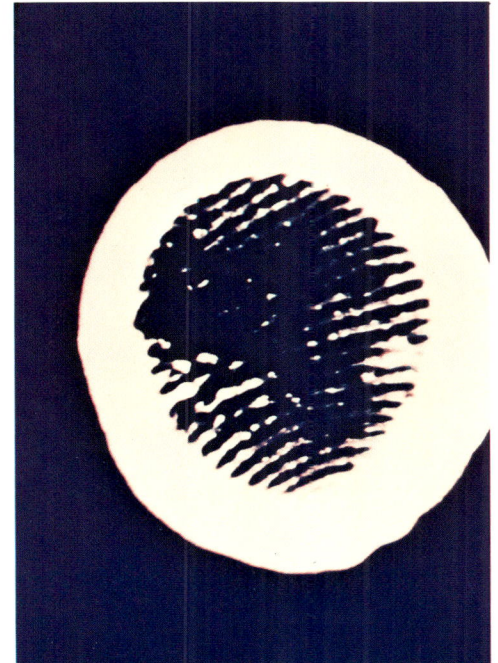
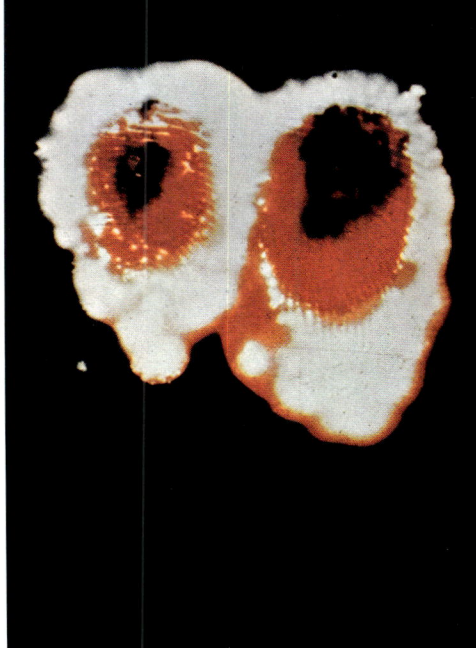

The New Technology

Cameras and Equipment

New 110 cameras from Kodak: Tele-Instamatic 608 (top) and Trimlite 48 (bottom)

The Adaptable 110

The quick popularity of the tiny, easy-to-use 110 camera prompted manufacturers to introduce several advanced models in 1975. Some of these have new features built into them; others are designed to accept a range of new accessories. In both cases these advanced models bring to 110 photography the versatility of larger format cameras.

One new accessory was a revolutionary 110 flash bulb unit *(page 162)* designed to reduce red reflections in the subject's eyes. To accommodate the flash unit, Kodak brought out its Trimlite series, consisting of four models. The most interesting and promising of these cameras is the top-of-the-line Trimlite 48, which not only accepts the new flash, but also features automatic exposure control, a four-element f/2.7 lens, and range-finder focusing to take the guesswork out of judging distances.

The Trimlite 48 also contains a lever in the film compartment which will adapt the camera's exposure control system to a type of high-speed film so new that when the camera first appeared the film was not yet on the market. The film, due to be introduced during 1976, enables 110 users to photograph in low-light situations without flash. With the lever, Trimlite 48 owners need merely to insert the new film for the camera to convert.

Agfa-Gevaert, the West German camera and film producer, has also added three new 110 models to its Agfamatic lines. All of them take the new flash bulb units. The most sophisticated of the three, the Agfamatic 4008, has an electronically controlled shutter with a range of speeds from 1/500 to 30 seconds. The 4008 can be focused to accommodate close-up portraits, middle-distance scenes and far-off landscapes. On all three of these Agfamatics, the shutter is cocked and the film advanced when the photographer pushes in and then pulls out the two-sectional body.

Another, and especially noteworthy, of the new 110s is Kodak's Tele-Instamatic 608, which contains two complete lens systems. Along with a normal 110 lens, a second lens with 72 per cent greater magnification than normal is built in. Sliding a switch shifts from the normal to the telephoto lens and, at the same time, indicates the new picture area in the viewfinder.

Sedic XF-22 with motor drive and flash attachments

The XP series of cameras from Hanimex and the Sedic XF series, both from Australia, bring to 110s for the first time the kinds of complementary attachments, designed for a specific camera body, that give such great flexibility to 35mm cameras. Both the XP and the XF series accept toylike, motor drive attachments that permit pictures to be taken at the rate of two frames per second. Close-up, wide-angle and telephoto supplemental lenses are also available for each camera. In addition, the top models—the Hanimex XP-3 and the Sedic XF-33 —have automatic exposure control and f/6.5 lenses.

The Contax RTS 35mm SLR

New Faces on the SLR

Five new models, which were introduced in 1975, add to the already impressive array of cameras available for the 35mm SLR enthusiast. Highest priced is the $800-plus Contax RTS, a joint venture of the Japanese industrial giant Yashica and one of the world's outstanding lens makers, Karl Zeiss of West Germany. Their collaboration has produced a professional instrument with automatic shutter control.

To take a picture with the Contax RTS, all the photographer has to do is focus, set the aperture and press the shutter button—an electronic rather than a mechanical trigger. The camera electronically selects the correct shutter speed. In an automatic operation, the shutter speed is flashed in the viewfinder by light-emitting diodes (LEDs) at the moment of exposure; but, the photographer can preview the camera-calculated shutter speed by pressing a button on the front of the camera body. When used under unusual lighting conditions or for special effects, the automatic exposure can be overridden.

Accessories for the Contax RTS encompass an array of bayonet-mount lenses and more than sixty other supplemental devices. Most interesting are motor drives for rapid shooting and specialized equipment for extreme close-ups.

Still another new-single lens reflex camera, the Miranda dx-3, introduces a unique device to facilitate accurate focusing: a dual system which combines a micro-prism and a split-image focuser. The microprism makes out-of-focus images appear fractured, and the image-

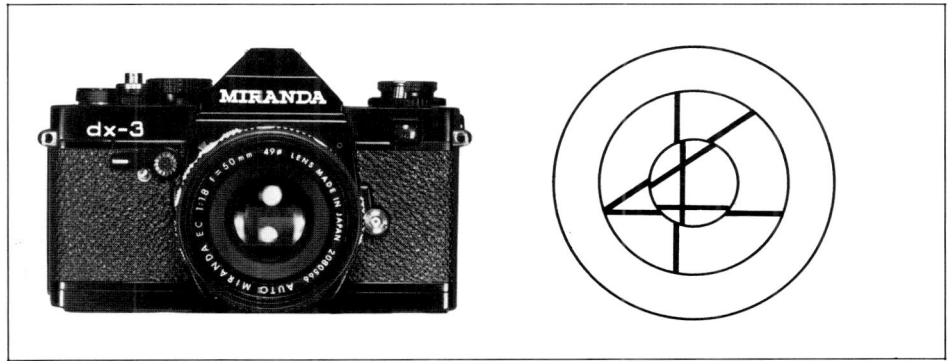

Miranda's dx-3 (above, left) and detail of dual-purpose viewfinder

splitter makes them out of alignment. When both conditions are corrected, sharp focus is assured. In addition, the image-splitter is circular so that any straight line in the image can be used for focusing.

Pentax and Minolta brought out 35mm SLR instruments with electronically controlled metal shutters. These shutters permit picture taking with an electronic flash at speeds up to 1/125 of a second, rather than the usual slower limit of 1/60 of a second—a speed that sometimes results in undesirable ghostlike images of moving subjects.

The Pentax camera with this feature is the K-2, the top model in the new K series. In this line, Pentax abandoned screw-mount lenses in favor of the easier-to-use bayonet mounts. On the automatic K-2, the f-number is selected and speed is set electronically.

An ultra-quiet metallic shutter, which reduces disturbing noise and vibration, is found on two Minolta models: the XE-7 (XE-1 outside the United States and Canada) and the XE-5. Both Minolta cameras have an automatic exposure system using a CdS cell meter. When taking a picture, the aperture is chosen, and the shutter speed is automatically set. Both Minoltas—and the Pentax—allow photographers to override the automatic setting and choose their own shutter speeds.

The New Technology/Cameras and Equipment

The fully automatic Bronica EC-TL

A Pair of Pioneers

Two medium-format cameras made news in 1975. One was the Bronica EC-TL, the first automatic 2¼ x 2¼-inch camera ever to hit the market. Its built-in electronic exposure system is as fully automated as that of the most sophisticated 35mm camera and its larger-film format has the advantage of fine-grained images. The EC-TL's appearance last year surprised many enthusiasts: they had thought the Rollei SLX would be the first automatic medium-format camera. But Rollei's internal financial problems inhibited the development and marketing of new products and introduction of their camera is not expected until mid-1976.

With the Bronica EC-TL's automatic exposure system, the photographer simply selects the aperture, focuses and presses the shutter release to take a picture. When the shutter release is depressed, the diaphragm closes down to the preselected aperture. Silicon photocells measure the brightness of the central portion of the image area and signal it to a tiny calculator, which determines the right shutter speed. The mirror then flips out of the way, and the focal-plane shutter exposes the film at the correct speed.

The shutter speed is indicated in the viewfinder at the moment of exposure. But the EC-TL has a preview control that allows the photographer to monitor the speed before the picture is taken and an override system if special effects require manual operation.

The new camera, conveniently enough, uses the same wide range of Nikkor lenses that were designed for older, nonautomated Bronicas. Interchangeable viewfinders, focusing screens and film backs are also available from Bronica.

The other new medium-format camera to cause a stir this year was the Mamiya M645. The camera revives the esthetically and economically attractive 2¼ x 1⅝-inch picture size—and in fact the camera's name derives from the metric equivalent of this format: 6 by 4.5 centimeters. This format was all but abandoned in the 1950s by medium-format film producers, who chose to emphasize the advantages of large picture size as a sales-generating alternative to 35mm photography.

But the shallower dimension of the new camera's images allow 15 shots to be made on one roll of 120 film, whereas most medium-format instruments, with their 2¼ x 2¼ images, can produce only 12. In addition, the images' proportions are much closer to those of standard enlarging paper than either the 35mm or 2¼-inch-square size. Thus, a smaller portion of the Mamiya image is lost during enlargement.

To make picture taking easier, the M645 has two shutter releases so that whether the camera is held vertically or horizontally a button is conveniently located at the photographer's fingertip. The Mamiya also comes equipped with an electron-

Mamiya's rectangular-format M645

ically timed but manually set shutter. When the accessory Mamiya PD viewfinder is added, however, its silicon-cell meter couples with the shutter-speed and aperture controls to provide a match system of metering. Other accessories include a whole range of lenses, four interchangeable focusing screens, and inexpensive film holders that can be preloaded and then quickly and easily dropped into the camera.

The $1,500 Rebikoff-Alpa U-Phot underwater camera

Underwater Gear

This year manufacturers responded to fast-rising interest in marine photography with two 35mm underwater cameras and two novel protective housings for cameras.

The most sophisticated of the new units is the $1,500 Rebikoff-Alpa U-Phot camera, designed primarily for professionals. The body of this 35mm camera is a cylinder 6 inches in diameter made of heavy-duty corrosion-resistant alloy. It will withstand water pressure at 300-foot depths—below which there is neither life nor light enough for photography. The U-Phot has automatic exposure control and a built-in, battery-powered motor drive to advance and rewind the film.

The CdS exposure system automatically sets the aperture to match a preselected shutter speed. Each of three shutter speeds—1/60, 1/125 and 1/300—can be synchronized with a watertight electronic flash, also available from U-Phot.

To eliminate the distortion normal to underwater photography, the U-Phot's wide-angle 35mm, f/2.8 lens is supplemented with a corrector lens; illuminated numbers count the number of exposures the photographer-diver has made.

For both professionals and serious amateurs, the other promising new article of equipment is the Nikonos III—the latest in Nikon's excellent line of underwater cameras. Like its predecessor, Nikonos II, this camera is a non-automated 35mm instrument, but with refinements in its design: a durable lens mount, easier-to-see shutter-speed dial and exposure counter, and an easier-to-use viewfinder and rewind crank. Another improvement is the

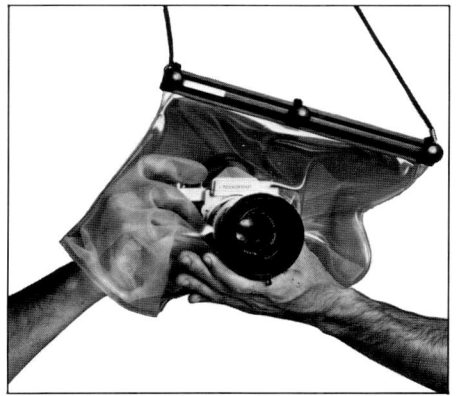
Spiratone's plastic sac for protecting a 35mm camera

addition of a sprocket wheel to advance film evenly.

The novice who wants to go underwater with his present, dry-land 35mm SLR camera can do so by encasing it in an inexpensive plastic housing called the Goedecke Ewa-Marine—distributed in the United States by Spiratone under the name Aqua Housing. The Ewa-Marine has glass ports for the lens and viewfinder; the photographer operates the camera through a built-in glove. Designed for depths to 30 feet, the

Ikelite's housing for Polaroid's SX-70 Land Camera

housing can also be used to protect a camera from rain, or from spray on a boat or at poolside.

Polaroid also found a way to go underwater in 1975. The Ikelite Underwater Systems developed a hard plastic housing which allows instant-developing color photographs with an SX-70 to be made at depths to 300 feet. All controls can be easily operated through the housing. After the picture is taken, a watertight pocket below the acrylic lens port catches the photograph as it is ejected from the camera, letting the photographer see what he has shot.

The New Technology/Cameras and Equipment

General Electric's flash unit for 110 cameras

Flexible Flashes

General Electric came out this year with a radically new flash-bulb unit designed for Kodak's new Trimlite and Tele-Instamatic 110 cameras *(page 158)*. The disposable unit, called FlipFlash, has two sets of four bulbs each, arranged in a tall, flat package that plugs into the top of the camera.

The bulbs in each set are connected by a circuit printed in conductive ink. When the flash unit is plugged into a camera, the circuit for the top four bulbs connects with the camera flash trigger. Pressing the shutter release will produce a pulse of high voltage within the camera that ignites one of the four bulbs in the top set.

The heat from the exploding bulb prepares the adjacent bulb for firing by, in effect, activating the portion of the printed circuit leading directly to it. When the second bulb flashes, it arms the third bulb in the same way, which in turn arms the fourth. After the first set of four bulbs has been used, the flash must be flipped over to put the unused bulbs on top. The five-inch height of FlipFlash assures that exploding bulbs are at least 3 inches above the lens, eliminating—without the use of a special extender—red reflections from a subject's eyes.

The Vivitar 283 flash (top) with lens holder and filters

Another innovation is Vivitar's versatile electronic flash Model 283. The basic unit contains an electrical circuit based on a thyristor, a type of transistor. The thyristor circuit automatically cuts off the power when just the right amount of light has been reflected from the subject for correct exposure. This automatic exposure control is possible at any of four f-stops.

The light sensor is detachable. An extension cord connecting with the flash unit allows the sensor to be mounted on the camera body so that no matter where the flash is aimed, the sensor is still directed toward the subject and reads the light hitting it. When the flash unit's movable head is tilted up for the softer effect of bounced light, the flash output is automatically boosted by the sensor to compensate for diffusion and absorption. The unit can be powered by four different sources —with alkaline batteries, quick recharging nickel-cadmium batteries, an AC adapter or a 510-volt battery pack for the rapid return of power after each flash.

A unique feature of the Vivitar 283 is an accessory bracket that allows a white reflector card to be clipped to the flash unit, providing a portable bounce surface. Other accessories include plastic lenses to spread the light for wide-angle shots or to concentrate the light when a telephoto is used. The lens holder will also accept filters to dim the flash or to change its color.

A Spectrum of New Lenses

The new lenses for 35mm cameras range from the specialized to the multifunctional. Of the former the most highly specialized is a portrait lens that deliberately blurs the image. Called the EBC Fujinon SF 85mm f/4 lens, it not only enables photographers to cast a hazy mist over portraits—and other images—but also lets them control the degree of haziness. This unusual effect occurs because light rays passing through the center of the lens and those coming through the edge of the lens focus at different points on the film, making a blurry image.

Most lenses are constructed of several elements that compensate for this condition, which is called spherical aberration. With the Fujinon at its widest aperture setting, the condition occurs unimpeded. However, by closing the aperture the photographer can cut off the edge rays and reduce blurriness—until, at any aperture setting of f/11 or smaller, the image that is produced is sharp.

Also specialized, although more

Vivitar's Macro lens and extender (at left)

versatile, are two new lenses from Vivitar and Nikon. Both these lenses are designed primarily to be used for close-up photography; each of them will also function as a telephoto lens to magnify objects at any given distance. When they are mounted directly onto a camera, both lenses are capable of handling close-up images of up to one-half of life size. And when they are used with an extender—a device that increases the distance between the lens and the film—both can produce life-sized pictures of subjects.

Because of a difference in the design of the two lenses, each of them must be supplemented by a different kind of extender for doing life-sized work. The special design of the Vivitar Series 1 90mm f/2.5 Macro requires that additional lenses be built inside the extender in order to focus with maximum effectiveness on close objects.

However, with the Nikon Micro-Nikkor 105mm f/4, no other lenses are needed in the extender; the tube simply functions as a way to increase the distance to the film.

Most versatile of the year's new lenses are zooms that go down into the wide-angle range—40mm and under. Among the zoom lenses that have this wide-angle capability are the 35mm to 105mm f/3.5 Asanuma Macro; the 35mm to 105mm f/3.5 Soligor C-D Macro; the 39mm to 80mm f/3.5 Sigma XQ Macro; the 40mm to 80mm f/2.8 MC Zoom Rokkor X; the 28mm to 45mm f/4.5 Zoom Nikkor; and the 38mm to 90mm f/3.5 Rokunar Macro, which is also sold under the Sun brand name.

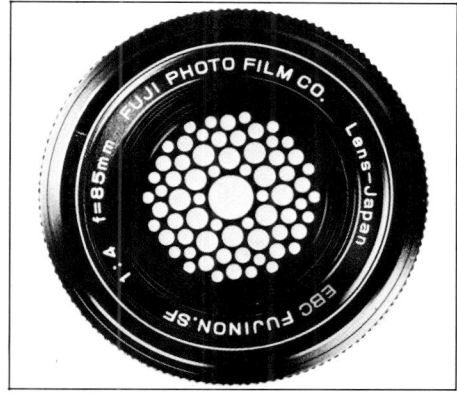
The Nikkor 105mm lens with extender attached

Another multifunctional lens with a wide-angle capability is Vivitar's Series 1 35mm to 85mm f/2.8. Called a varifocal lens, it is not a true zoom lens because, as the magnification changes, the focus must be readjusted in order to keep the image clear. However, it gives nearly the versatility of and is considerably more compact and light in weight than are comparable zooms.

Fuji's soft-focus portrait lens

The New Technology/Cameras and Equipment

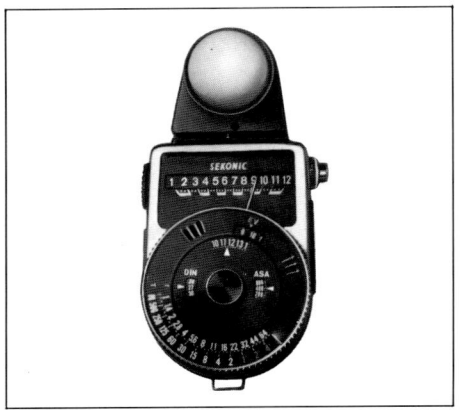

Sekonic's hand-held silicon cell light meter

Hand Meters with Silicon Cells

Two hand-held light meters—the Bewi-Zoom-Spot and the Sekonic L-428—came on the market equipped with quick-reacting light sensors of silicon. Previously, hand meters had contained cells of cadmium sulfide (CdS); the new meters, with their silicon cells, react more quickly to light, and they do not carry any "memory." That is, they do not retain slow-fading impressions from previous readings to distort a new one, as occurs with CdS meters.

The Bewi-Zoom, though designed for spot readings, can increase its angle of view. Through a viewfinder, a photographer can see that the meter is reading light in an area covering an angle from 7° to 35°. And, squeezing a trigger, he can zero in to read light in a range from 1° to 5°. This flexibility is especially useful with telephoto lenses.

By the interchange of accessories, the Sekonic L-428 can be used not only for spot work, but also for average-reflected and incident-light readings. The addition of a lens makes it a spot meter. With a diffusing sphere attached, the L-428 becomes an incident-light meter, measuring the light falling on a subject when the meter is held next to it. With a light filter, it is a reflected light meter aimed at a subject to read the light bouncing off it. Other accessories will adapt the meter for movies and photomicrography.

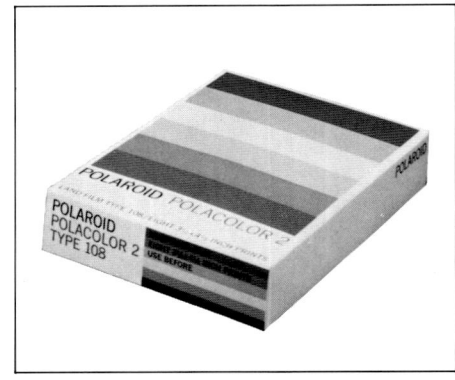

Polaroid's improved color print film

Improvement in Polacolor

Instant color film technology took a step forward in 1975 when Polaroid introduced Polacolor 2 for its own 3¼ x 4¼-inch film-pack cameras and for other cameras designed for Polaroid film packs. Based on dyes developed for the SX-70 Land film system, each sheet of film in the eight-sheet pack has a multilayer emulsion, with the dyes chemically structured to protect colors from the ultraviolet rays that cause fading. Also, the base material is not so apt to curl as is other Polaroid film.

Darkroom Helper

A device for checking the focus of images on the enlarger easel takes much of the strain out of darkroom work. The foot-tall Unicolor-Mitchell Focusing Aide has a ground-glass screen large enough to be viewed easily by the home printer when standing at the easel. This design is a great advantage when the enlarger head is raised to the top of the post—sometimes four feet above the supporting table—to create an oversize enlargement. The focuser reduces the stretching a printmaker must go through to adjust the enlarger while trying at the same time to keep an eye on the image.

Moreover, the new device is pointed and can be tilted to check image sharpness at the edges of a print, where enlarger light falls at extreme angles. Fixed focusers cannot tilt to capture light at such extreme angles.

The convenient Unicolor-Mitchell focusing aide

The Annual Awards /6

# The Annual Awards /6

Something Old, Something New 168

Sports Photographer of the Year—Great Britain

Britain's Royal Photographic Society and the Sports Council gave their joint award for a portfolio of daring parachute pictures that included this remarkable view of free-fall jumpers, 8,000 feet over North Carolina, joining hands in a maneuver known as making a star. The photographer, a champion skydiver who has represented Great Britain in international competition, took this picture with a camera attached to his helmet as he plummeted toward the earth at 120 miles per hour.

DAVE WATERMAN: *Birds of a Feather,* 1973

The Annual Awards

Something Old, Something New

Vintage photographs and low-key news pictures take the lion's share of this year's prizes

In a year filled with surprises, photography's past and present mingled improbably in the array of pictures that won top prizes. Alongside stunning examples of the present state of the art were pictures taken years or even decades ago. For example, Jean-Louis Nou's dramatic picture of the ritual cremation of a Brahman elder on page 181 was taken in 1966, and Kineo Kuwahara's photograph of a dollmaker's show window *(page 171)* is part of a pre-World War II documentary that did not appear in book form until 1974.

There were other unexpected awards this year, particularly among those given for photojournalism. The Robert Capa award specifies that the photographer must exercise "exceptional courage and enterprise," virtually guaranteeing that winning photographs will be bloody and violent. But this year's Capa Gold Medal was given to W. Eugene Smith *(page 182)* for a compassionate essay on industrial pollution victims in Japan; in the process of getting his pictures, Smith was brutally beaten and nearly blinded by industry thugs. A new wave is sweeping newspaper photography in the United States moving it away from stereotypes of action and violence toward more quiet, personal scenes, and riding the crest is Pat Crowe. He became Newspaper Photographer of the Year not with sensational front-page pictures but with a sensitive portfolio that included a backstage portrait of a circus clown putting on his make-up *(page 175)*. And although a fire picture won a Pulitzer prize for Jerry Gay, the winner was a quiet image of exhausted firemen *(page 183)*, not a spectacular shot of the fire itself.

By far the greatest surprise among the prize winners came from Europe, where not one but hundreds of thousands of photographers won West Germany's prestigious *Kulturpreis*. The award was given nominally to the German Red Cross for its 30-year effort to trace almost two million Germans listed as missing at the end of World War II. To aid the search, the Red Cross assembled 900,000 snapshots from old army ID cards and family albums. They were published in a 199-volume work—one page appears on page 180—and entire sets of these books were distributed around the Continent. As a result, many men have been reunited with their families since the war, many more thousands have been confirmed as dead, and the Red Cross's legion of anonymous photographers—the ultimate winners of the *Kulturpreis*—have established an indelible record of the face of a destroyed army.

Nendo Sho (Annual Award)—Japan

On the wintry shore of Japan's Izumo Province the gateway to a Shinto shrine rises against a bleak backdrop of snow, sea and sky. This perception of symmetry and mood earned a coveted Nendo Sho from the Japan Photography Society—whose other award winners are presented on the following five pages.

SHOJI UEDA: *Izumo,* 1953

The Annual Awards/**Something Old, Something New**

SHOMEI TOMATSU: *The Pencil of the Sun,* 1973

Nendo Sho (Annual Award)—Japan

Her knotty feet planted firmly on the floor of her hut, a spry old peasant gestures to her visitor to have a seat. The photographer, a freelancer, spent six months on a tiny island off Okinawa, recording the lives of the 20 families of farmers and fishermen living there. The result, which includes this lively characterization, he fancifully titled The Pencil of the Sun.

Nendo Sho (Annual Award)—Japan

This arresting shot of a dollmaker's show window is one of a collection, recently come to light, taken before World War II in the poorer districts of Tokyo. After taking the picture, Kuwahara discovered that the dollmaker, often berated by his wife for being drunk, had made this life-sized doll of himself as a snoozing drunkard and stuck it in the window.

KINEO KUWAHARA: *The House of the Dollmaker,* 1937

The Annual Awards/**Something Old, Something New**

Nendo Sho (Annual Award)—Japan

Musashino, the title of a picture book, is also the name of a plain west of Tokyo whose natural beauties the photographer has aimed to preserve on film before they succumb to urbanization. Among the scenes is this bamboo thicket; its columns form a somber palisade that seems to guard the sun-drenched sanctum against the encroachment of developers.

TAKEYOSHI TANUMA: *Musashino*, 1969

Shinjin Sho (Newcomer Award) —Japan

The Japan Photography Society's Newcomer Award for special achievement by a relatively unknown photographer went for this fresh approach to the much-photographed city of Kyoto and its temples. Using double exposure, Yamamura first photographed the wooden colonnade of a Buddhist temple; then for his second image he turned to the ornate roof tiles overhead as melting snow ran off in streams.

KUNIO YAMAMURA: *Picture Tales of Kyoto,* 1974

The Annual Awards/**Something Old, Something New**

TAKUYA TSUKAHARA: *White Play,* 1971

Nendo Sho (Annual Award)—Japan

To the photographer, the sterile space he had created in his studio was meant to suggest the barrenness of the modern world. For his four-year-old models, however, it was an ideal playroom. Their spontaneous antics, photographed through a peephole, resulted in a surreal scene of childish fun and games.

Newspaper Photographer of the Year —U.S.A.

Ringling Brothers' famous dwarf-clown Paul Alpert sends puffs of powder flying as he slaps on makeup before going under the big top. The award, won by a Wilmington, Delaware, News-Journal photographer, is sponsored by a consortium of the National Press Photographers Association, the University of Missouri School of Journalism and Nikon, Inc.; the same group also gives the Magazine Photographer of the Year Award shown on page 177.

PAT CROWE: *Prince Paul*, 1974

The Annual Awards/**Something Old, Something New**

Le Prix Nadar—France
This photograph of a wounded United States marine in Vietnam reaching compassionately toward a stricken comrade is characteristic of those in the volume Vu par LIFE (the French title for The Best of LIFE), which won the prize of the Association des Gens d'Image for the best picture book brought out in France in the previous year. The photographer was later killed in a helicopter over Laos.

LARRY BURROWS: *Untitled*, 1966

**Magazine Photographer of the Year
—U.S.A.**

On a swing through the Middle East during the oil crisis, photographer Adams of TIME portrayed Egypt's President Anwar Sadat exuding Arab bonhomie as he chatted, wearing traditional peasant garb, with neighbors outside a mosque in his village birthplace.

EDDIE ADAMS: *Anwar Sadat,* 1974

The Annual Awards/**Something Old, Something New**

**Pulitzer Prize for
Feature Photography—U.S.A.**
*This portrait of 70-year-old British riding master Major John Lynch was one of a series of studies that captured for Washington Post photographer Lewis the first Pulitzer Prize ever given to a portfolio of color pictures.
As the portrait was taken, Lynch, then running a riding academy in Leesburg, Virginia, beamingly recalled the days when he trained mounts for the royal family in England.*

MATTHEW LEWIS: *Major John Lynch,* 1974

Best Press Contributions of the Year—U.S.S.R.

To the applause of fellow workers in a Siberian oil town, a couple seal their 50th wedding anniversary with an embrace. The photograph conveys an earthy Russian camaraderie that undoubtedly recommended it to the Union of Soviet Journalists, sponsor of the annual award.

VSEVOLOD TARASEVICH: *The Golden Kiss*, 1974

The Annual Awards/**Something Old, Something New**

UNKNOWN PHOTOGRAPHERS: *Missing German Soldiers, World War II*

Kulturpreis—Germany

On the 30th anniversary of World War II's end, the German Society for Photography gave its prize collectively to the nameless photographers who contributed to the German Red Cross's 199-volume collection of snapshots showing the 1.74 million Germans reported missing during the war. This sample page shows a group of men known to have been in the same Russian prison camp. The "X" marks, stamped on by hand since the books' publication in 1966, indicate either that the man has since been found—or is known to have perished.

Le Prix Niepce—France

In a rarely photographed scene, which earned Nou the year's promising newcomer award from the Association des Gens d'Image, Brahman villagers in southern India gather in a clearing for the funeral of an elder. The body, shrouded in white cotton, is being laid on a funeral pyre of split logs, prepared by the two workmen in the foreground (left and right). The corpse will be drenched with kerosene and set alight to the chants of the mourners.

JEAN-LOUIS NOU: *Cremation in Kerala, India*, 1966

The Annual Awards/**Something Old, Something New**

World Understanding Award—U.S.A.
Robert Capa Gold Medal—U.S.A.
On the Japanese island of Kyushu a mother tenderly bathes her daughter, 16, grotesquely deformed and blind since birth from mercury poisoning. The photograph is from a series on industrial pollution by W. Eugene Smith and his wife Aileen, for which they jointly received the World Understanding Award. Gene Smith, who was severely beaten by goons hired by the offending chemical company, also received the Robert Capa award for "photography requiring exceptional courage and enterprise."

W. EUGENE SMITH: *Minamata, Japan,* 1971

**Pulitzer Prize for
Spot News Photography—U.S.A.**

These firemen battled flames for three solid hours, but the fire got out of hand and the house they were trying to save in Burien, Washington, burned to the ground. Now, in the early morning they are resting amid muck and smoke, a picture of sodden dejection that speaks eloquently of the exhausting—and frequently heartbreaking—business of firefighting.

JERRY GAY: *Lull in the Battle,* 1974

The Annual Awards/**Something Old, Something New**

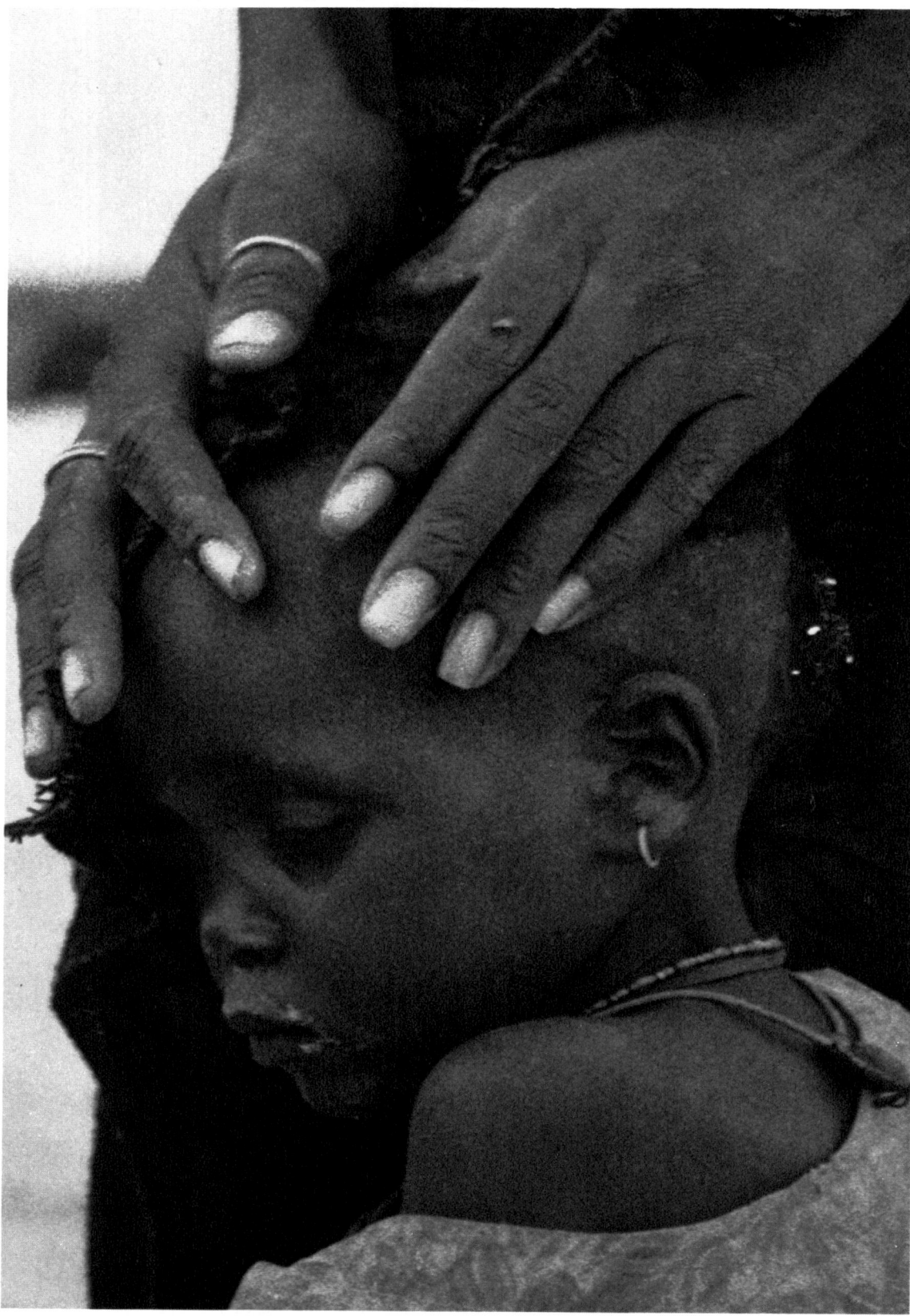

OVIE CARTER: "Suffer little children," 1974

**Press Photo of the Year Award—
The Netherlands
Pulitzer Prize for International
Reporting—U.S.A.**

In a moving symbol of maternal love, a tribal woman in drought-stricken Niger places her hands protectively on her starving four-year-old. The picture was taken during a 10,000-mile trek across the hunger belt of Africa and Asia— the first foreign assignment for the young black photographer. Carter got the Netherlands' Award for this picture, and shared the Pulitzer with reporter William Mullen who accompanied him.

The Year's Books /7

The Year's Books / 7

Melancholy Shantytown	188
Dazzling Slide Show	196
Cryptic Impressions	200
A Romance with America	208
Other Books	214

Romance with America/ ERNST HAAS: *Vintage Model T Ford on a Country Road Near Knoxville, Tennessee,* 1962

The Year's Books

Melancholy Shantytown

The harsh fate of Gypsies languishing in segregated settlements is the subject of Josef Koudelka's impassioned study

GYPSIES
Photographs by Josef Koudelka.
Text by Willy Guy. Unnumbered pages. Aperture, Inc., Millerton, New York, 1975. $22.50.

The Gypsies in Josef Koudelka's stark photographs stare out of the page with melancholy eyes that seem to say, "We have reached the end of the road." They are not the colorful wanderers of popular legend, pursuing a carefree life in brightly painted caravans. They are not even the motorized travelers of today who now roam the roads of Europe and America in automobiles and vans. They are, on the contrary, the settled Gypsies of Czechoslovakia's easternmost province, where Gypsies were forced to give up roaming and settle down into small segregated communities.

Koudelka himself is a Czech, a 38-year-old former aeronautical designer who first became interested in Gypsies when stationed among them during his military service. He has spent more than 10 years photographing Gypsies all over Europe, studying their history and culture as he traveled among them with only a light backpack and his two Leicas.

In *Gypsies,* his first book published outside his native country, he gives a documentary study of shantytown life, not a romance of the open road. The pictures are somber: posed portraits lit like Old Master paintings alternating with more casual candid shots of everyday life.

The settled Gypsies of East Slovakia live in rural shantytowns, sometimes miles from the nearest village; they subsist on odd jobs or government doles. They have long since abandoned their colorful Gypsy garb, and dress the way poor people dress everywhere, in cheap, anonymous clothes with nothing about them that expresses the human beings they enclose.

The luckier ones, like the three part-time factory workers shown on the facing page, live in houses abandoned by the Germans who were forced to leave Czechoslovakia after World War II. At the opposite extreme is the one-room shack of two young women on page 190—one of whom has inexplicably removed her blouse for Koudelka's camera. More typical is the interior of the house belonging to the two elderly pensioners on page 191; the stucco walls are whitewashed, and its occupants have used a stick dipped in paint to make the decorative pattern on the wall.

Although Koudelka can show the cheerful side of Gypsy life—children playing in the street and musicians at a party—melancholy seems the inescapable essence of his book. He reflects the Gypsies' preoccupation with death and the ceremonies attending it. The dead lie in state for three days and nights before the funeral while the relatives and family friends keep watch, drinking, telling stories and praying. Then the bodies are carried in procession from the settlement to the nearest church for a mass before proceeding to the graveyard. The photograph on page 195 might stand for the whole book: an ancient ritual of mourning is observed—a dead girl's eyes are covered with coins—as an image of the Holy Mother looks down on the living and the dead alike.

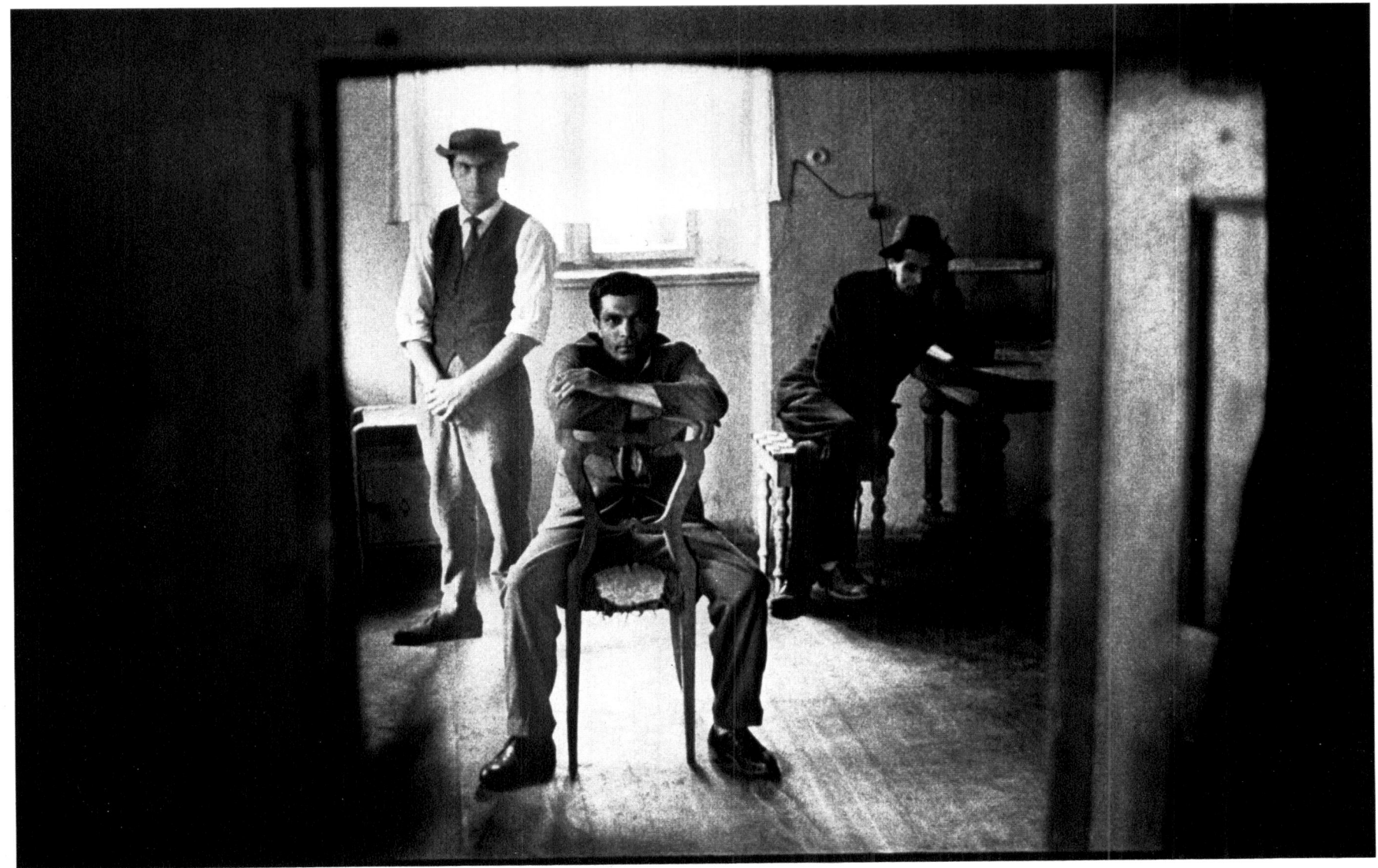
Gypsy Textile Workers, Kadan, 1962

The Year's Books/**Koudelka's Shantytown**

Two Women, Vinodol, 1968

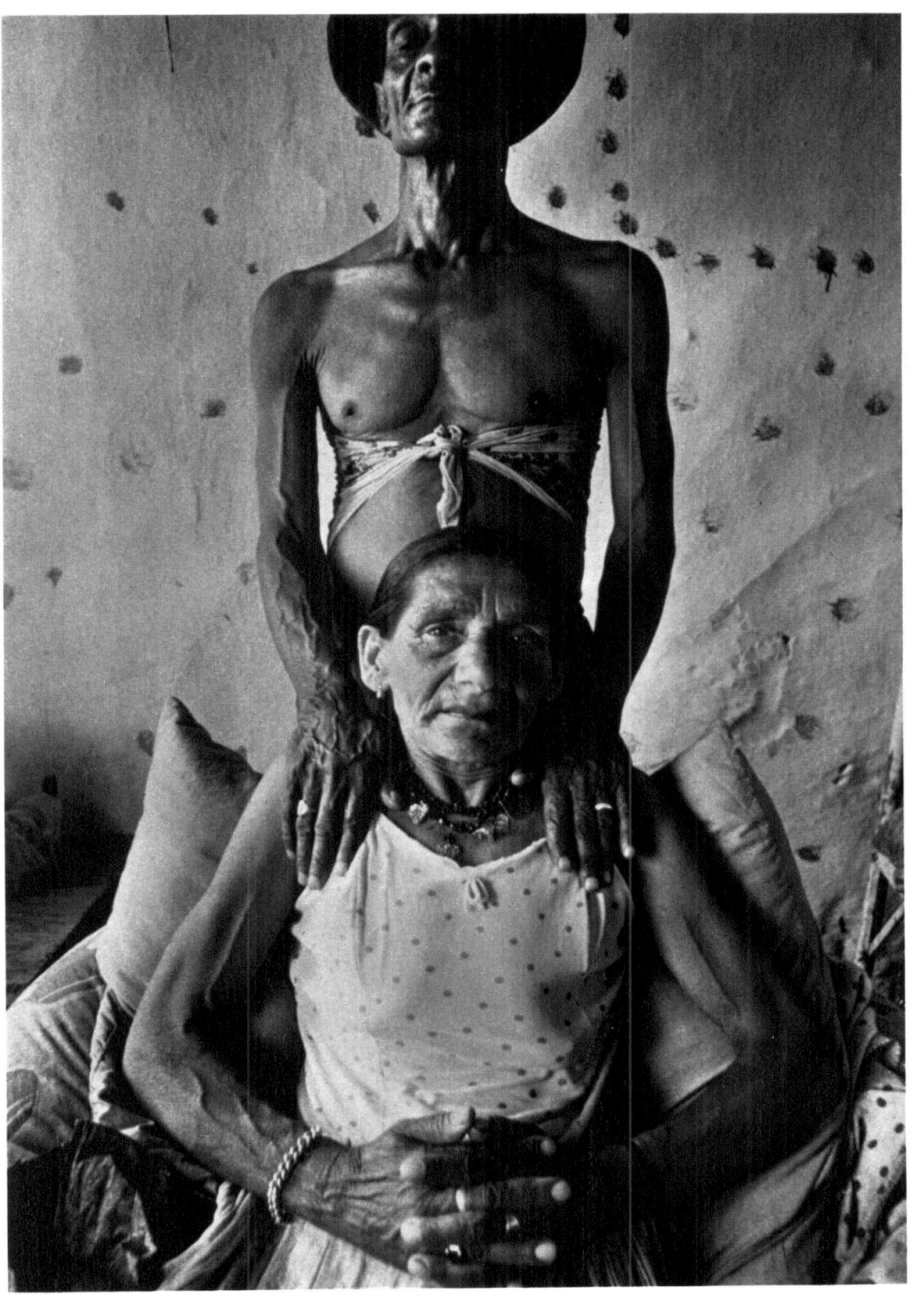

Gypsy Couple in Their Home, Zehra, 1967

The Year's Books/**Koudelka's Shantytown**

Sliding on Ice, Rakusy, 1964

Young Gypsy Men Playing for Dancers, Velka Lomnica, 1963

The Year's Books/**Koudelka's Shantytown**

Funeral for a Young Woman, Jarabina, 1963

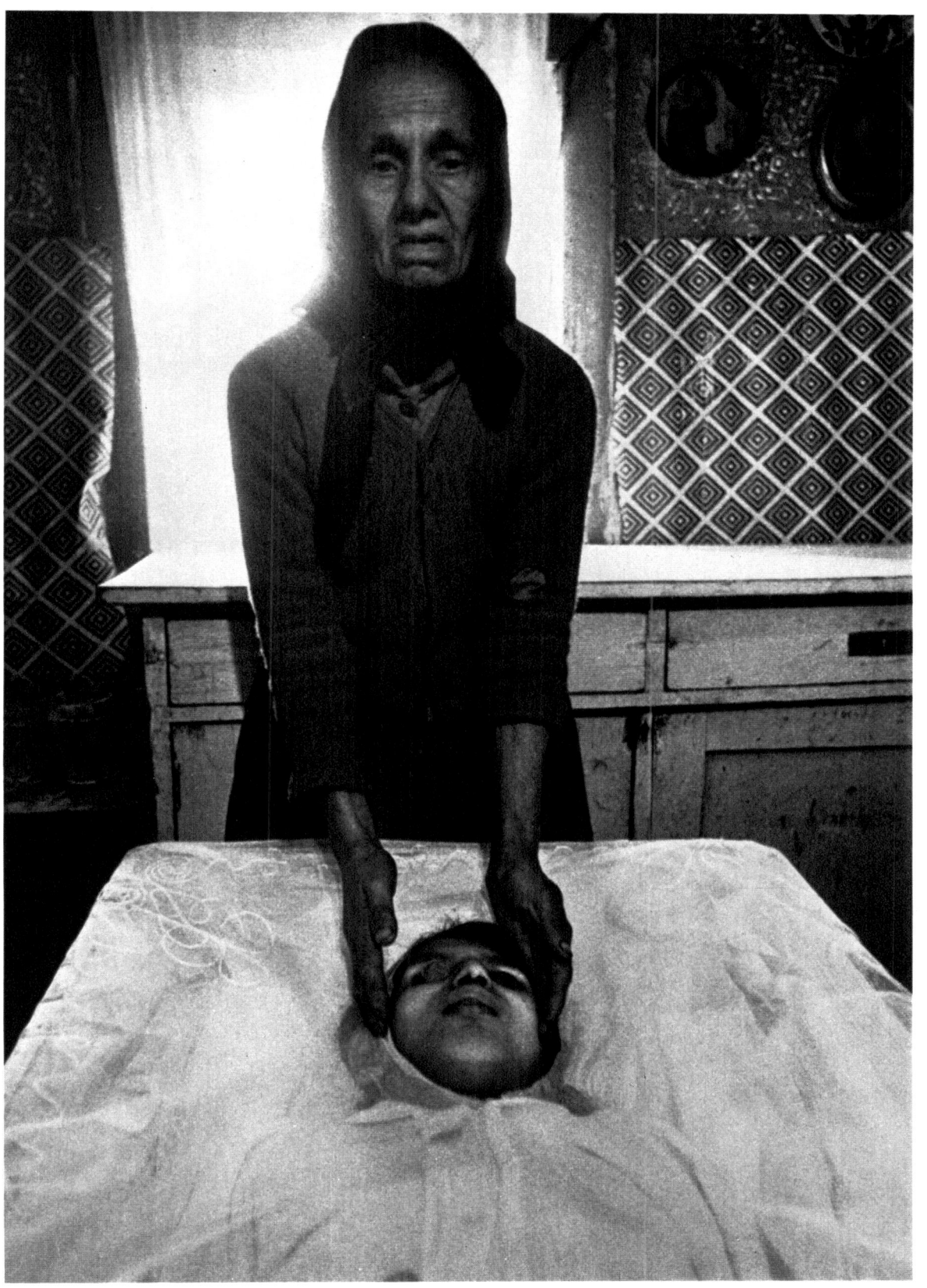

Woman Caressing Dead Grandchild Whose Eyes Are Covered by Coins, Bardejov, 1967

The Year's Books

A Dazzling Slide Show

In this fast-paced volume, Kishin Shinoyama restlessly switches subject matter and camera techniques

A FINE DAY
By Kishin Shinoyama. Unnumbered pages. Heibonsha, Tokyo, 1975. 5,000 yen (about $17).

Simply to open Kishin Shinoyama's sixth and latest book, *A Fine Day,* is an eye-filling experience. Without preamble of any kind—no introduction, no title page—the book presents the first of Shinoyama's compelling color photographs of 23 events that attracted widespread attention in Japan in 1974. As many as 18 pictures are devoted to each event. Subjects shift suddenly from baseball games to earthquakes, like a well-planned slide show. Within each sequence—and from one sequence to the next—Shinoyama creates a contrapuntal rhythm by juxtaposing subjects and techniques to emphasize both their similarities and differences in color, shape, style and mood.

In the book's opening sequence, shown in part in the top row opposite, a sailboat returning to Tokyo after a 275-day trip around the world first appears as a distant dot on the vast Pacific. Then, as Shinoyama's airborne camera circles and changes perspective, the boat jumps erratically closer until at last the viewer encounters the boat's skipper in a grainy enlargement. In another sequence *(middle and bottom rows),* Shinoyama uses a different camera treatment to cover the action of a prize fight: unrelenting closeups, each filling an entire double-page spread, provide a series of dramatically contrasting angles. Right after the final fight picture, the photographer humorously juxtaposes on facing pages a glaringly mis-lit Mona Lisa, from a display at the Tokyo National Museum, with a sultry night club singer.

"I had no overall or specific plan of action," Shinoyama says of the book. "I would develop a sudden interest in some event and then I would be off to take pictures." Such an intuitive approach does not produce the flawless elegance that is the aim of many Japanese photographers. But Shinoyama seems more interested in the graphic immediacy of his pictures and the swirling visual currents that a series of them creates. This approach was formulated during the 34-year-old photographer's apprenticeship in advertising photography, where variety, impact and storytelling are essentials. Now working on his own—and in constant demand for editorial and commercial assignments—Shinoyama chooses decidedly contemporary themes, which show postwar Japan as a modern nation with the same tastes, trends and problems as other industrialized countries.

For example, Shinoyama devotes one sequence to Japan's new breed of campaigning politicians, and several to its long-established passion for baseball. In his coverage of the national high school baseball playoffs *(middle row, overleaf),* he counterpoints shots of action on the field with closeups of applauding young fans and a cheerleader on the sidelines. The book's final sequence parallels in technique the yacht series that opens the book. Shinoyama's camera spots a gray speck in a lavender field; as it approaches it grows into the looming silhouette of an American F4 Phantom jet, belching smoke during a dummy nuclear bomb raid over Okinawa.

Shinoyama's Slide Show

The Year's Books

An Album of Cryptic Impressions

Jerry N. Uelsmann invites viewers to apply their own interpretations to a book of dreamlike composites

SILVER MEDITATIONS
By Jerry N. Uelsmann. Introduction by Peter C. Bunnell. 160 pages. Morgan & Morgan, Inc., Dobbs Ferry, N.Y., 1975. $14.95.

If the camera cannot lie, it tells a very strange truth in *Silver Meditations,* a new book of photographs by Jerry N. Uelsmann. Trees trail their roots through a landscape of mountains. Above a frieze of lips forming a smile, alligators seem to approach an entranceway to a university building. A neat bundle of rope floats in a white painted coffin in front of a country church. The creator of these cryptic images offers few clues to their meaning; they are deliberately mysterious.

Clearly Uelsmann's photographs are tricks conjured in the darkroom by combining elements from several negatives. Working with as many as five enlargers, Uelsmann prints parts of several negatives on the same paper. Sometimes he prints one image on top of another, giving the effect of a double exposure (as with the gigantic seedpod, in the water below the floating trees on page 205). At other times he produces a mirror image by taking two negatives of the same subject, flopping one, and joining them seamlessly on the printing paper (the trees in Totemic Aspen, page 204). Often he prints several different images edge to edge, hiding the joint between the negatives in a dark area (the fountain and basking alligators in *Welcome to Higher Education,* right).

Uelsmann makes no secret of his methods, which oppose the purist dictum, espoused by such photographers of an earlier generation as Edward Weston, Ansel Adams and Minor White, that the finished picture must be nothing more than what the photographer sees in his viewfinder when he snaps the shutter. On the contrary, Uelsmann glories in creating pictures that could not even be imagined, much less visualized, until he begins working in the darkroom using techniques based on those employed by Victorian masters of combination printing, such as O. G. Rejlander and H. P. Robinson.

Uelsmann's darkroom manipulations make hauntingly beautiful pictures that are more like photographs of a dream than of the real world. In the enigmatic picture on page 206, the photographer is seen through receding doors crouched over his tripod, his back to the viewer. Next to him, a split nut in the gaping hole of a tree trunk stares out like a camera lens. Nature's camera seems to be aimed at the viewer while the real photographer ignores him. In another example of Uelsmann's puzzling, and often humorous, art *(page 202),* four empty wooden lawn chairs are drawn up on a beach as if to watch the sun set over the ocean. But where the sun should be, shooting out sunbeams from a bank of clouds, there floats instead a gigantic hot dog—with mustard and relish. Some critics have seen this as a satire on the American Dream, which promises golden sunsets but delivers short-order food.

Interpreting Uelsmann's pictures is difficult, but that seems part of his message. "The viewer cannot be passive," says the photographer. "He must actively participate."

Welcome to Higher Education, 1974

The Year's Books/**Uelsmann's Impressions**

Untitled, 1971

Untitled, 1971

The Year's Books/**Uelsmann's Impressions**

Totemic Aspen, 1970

Untitled, 1969

The Year's Books/**Uelsmann's Impressions**

Untitled, 1973

Untitled, 1968

The Year's Books

A Romance with America

Austrian-born Ernst Haas uses vibrant color to celebrate the beauty — and the 200th birthday — of his adopted country

IN AMERICA
By Ernst Haas. 144 pages. A Studio Book/The Viking Press, New York, 1975. $42.50.

It was "entirely by chance," says Ernst Haas, that his book *In America* was ready for publication in the Bicentennial year of the United States. But the accident was a lucky one, for Haas's first book since his 1971 bestseller *The Creation* is a handsome celebration of the country's enduring beauty. Though all the photographs were taken after the 1950s, Haas managed to spice his book with touches of the more distant past through clever and judicious views of old buildings, old costumes and customs, and accurate simulations of various artifacts that had been created for movie sets. In viewing the present, Haas does not altogether ignore urban blight and the proliferation of roadside gas stations and motels and shops that threaten the beauty of the countryside. But his approach is basically affirmative and his book looks optimistically at such varied splendors as the Grand Canyon, New Orleans' Mardi Gras, the New England Fife and Drum Festival and a sailing regatta at the base of Mount Rainier.

Like many lovers of America, Haas is foreign born. He first achieved fame in his native Austria with a picture essay on the return of Austria's World War II prisoners. After a two-year stay in Paris he moved to the United States in 1950. He photographed numerous color essays for LIFE magazine and in 1962 held a one-man show at The Museum of Modern Art in New York City.

As a successful photojournalist and advertising photographer, Haas has learned to communicate his pictorial ideas clearly and effectively. In photographing a reconstructed pirate ship at Disneyland in California, he wished to convey the fantasies that thoughts of old sailing ships bestir in people today. To emphasize the vessel's remoteness from the present, Haas's picture shows the ship's reflection in a pool of water and not the ship itself.

Not surprisingly, New York City is one of Haas's favorite places. It is the subject of his most famous LIFE essays—a series of abstractions that appeared in 1953—and is also the photographer's home. Haas, long since become citywise, uses New York for a wide range of themes. Perhaps the most unexpected is the photograph of a rider on a bucking horse that appears on page 210; reminiscent of the Wild West, it was actually photographed in downtown Manhattan, at a Madison Square Garden rodeo.

Haas has never ceased to be surprised by the extremes between which everything from the weather to moral opinion oscillates in the United States. His sense of contrast is conveyed by two photographs *(pages 212 and 213)* of an old mansion near New Orleans and a main street in Albuquerque, New Mexico. Softly lit Corinthian columns are framed by shadowy out-of-focus foliage. By contrast, the photograph of glaring signs and buildings of a commercial thoroughfare in Albuquerque is as sharp and clear as a comic strip. But both are part of the endlessly varied and colorful pageant that Ernst Haas finds in his travels about the United States.

Disneyland Pirate Ship Reflected in a Pool, Anaheim, California, 1960

The Year's Books/**Haas in America**

Rodeo, Madison Square Garden, New York City, 1970

Boys Playing Handball, New York City, 1974

The Year's Books/**Haas in America**

Mansion near New Orleans, 1961

Central Avenue, Albuquerque, New Mexico, 1972

Other Books

The Editors recommend the following additional photography books published in 1975.

Current Work

CAN'T ARGUE WITH SUNRISE: A PAPER MOVIE
By Lou Stoumen. Celestial Arts, Millbrae, Calif. 192 pages. Hardbound, $14.95; softbound, $9.45. Still pictures from a documentary film-maker.

CHOSEN LAND:
THE SABBATHDAY LAKE SHAKERS
By Stephen Guion Williams. Afterword by Sister Mildred Barker. David R. Godine, Boston. Unnumbered pages. $12.50. Studies of a religious sect in rural Maine.

CIRCUS DAYS
By Jill Freedman. Harmony Books/Crown Publishers, New York. 128 pages. Hardbound, $12.95; softbound, $6.95. Life in a traveling tent show.

THE COWBOY
By Bank Langmore, text by Ron Tyler. William Morrow and Company, Inc., New York. 252 pages. $19.95. Color photographs of men on the modern-day range.

LONDONERS
By Nancy Hellebrand. Lund Humphries, London, England. (Distributed by Light Impressions, Rochester, N.Y.) 52 pages. $8.50. Portraits of Londoners in their homes.

MINAMATA
By W. Eugene Smith and Aileen M. Smith. An Alskog/Sensorium Book/Holt, Rinehart and Winston, New York. 192 pages. $10.00. Reportage on the effects of mercury poisoning on a Japanese village.

MOMENTS WITHOUT PROPER NAMES
By Gordon Parks. A Studio Book/The Viking Press, New York. 176 pages. $22.50. Samplings from the work of a renowned photojournalist.

OUR KIND OF PEOPLE:
AMERICAN GROUPS AND RITUALS
By Bill Owens. Straight Arrow Books, San Francisco. Unnumbered pages. $9.95. Civic and social groups in a suburban community.

THE PHOTOGRAPHER'S CHOICE: A BOOK OF PORTFOLIOS AND CRITICAL OPINION
Edited by Kelly Wise. Addison House, Danbury, N.H. (Distributed by Light Impressions, Rochester, N.Y.) 250 pages. Hardbound, $25.00; softbound, $12.95. Fresh selections from the work of 28 photographers.

SIDETRIPPING
By Charles Gatewood, text by William Burroughs. Strawberry Hill Publishing Company, Inc., New York. Unnumbered pages. $6.95. A stark view of 1970's America.

WASHINGTON SQUARE
By André Kertész. Introduction by Brendan Gill. Grossman Publishers, New York. Unnumbered pages. $5.95. Scenes and faces from New York's Greenwich Village.

WOMEN AND OTHER VISIONS
By Judy Dater and Jack Welpott. Introduction by Henry Holmes Smith. Morgan & Morgan, Inc., Dobbs Ferry, N.Y. Unnumbered pages. $14.95. Portraits of women, formal and erotic.

Retrospectives

JULIA MARGARET CAMERON:
HER LIFE AND PHOTOGRAPHIC WORKS
Arranged and written by Helmut Gernsheim. Aperture, Inc., Millerton, N.Y. 200 pages. $20.00. An illustrated biography of the famed Victorian photographer.

ERA OF EXPLORATION: THE RISE OF LANDSCAPE PHOTOGRAPHY IN THE AMERICAN WEST, 1860-1885
Compiled and written by Weston J. Naef, James N. Wood and Therese Thau Heyman. Distributed by New York Graphic Society, Boston. 260 pages. $25.00. Five photographers who documented the opening of the West.

THE LIGHT OF OTHER DAYS:
IRISH LIFE AT THE TURN OF THE CENTURY IN THE PHOTOGRAPHS OF ROBERT FRENCH
Edited by Kieran Hickey. David R. Godine, Boston. 172 pages. $22.50. Urban and pastoral Ireland by a Dublin photographer.

GEORGE A. TICE: PHOTOGRAPHS 1953-1973
Introduction by Lee Witkin. Rutgers University Press, Brunswick, N.J. 127 pages. Hardbound, $20.00; softbound, $12.50. Spare scenes from cities, woodlands and rural outposts.

Reprints

MAN RAY: PHOTOGRAPHS 1920-1934
Introduction by A. D. Coleman. East River Press, New York. 104 pages. $8.50. A collection of portraits, photograms and nudes by the premier Surrealist photographer; first printed in 1934.

NAKED CITY
By Weegee. Da Capo Press, New York. 243 pages. $12.95. New York City. A trend-setting press photographer's first book; originally brought out in 1945.

YOU HAVE SEEN THEIR FACES
By Margaret Bourke-White, text by Erskine Caldwell. An Arno Press Book/Derbibooks, Inc., New York. 190 pages. $6.95. The erosion of land and people in the Southern United States; first printed in 1937.

WALKER EVANS: AMERICAN PHOTOGRAPHS
Afterword by Lincoln Kirstein. East River Press, New York. 192 pages. $7.50. An album compiled by Evans of his finest photographs from the Depression years.

Historical

THE ILLUSTRATED HISTORY OF THE CAMERA FROM 1839 TO THE PRESENT
By Michel Auer. Translated and adapted by D. B. Tubbs. New York Graphic Society, Boston. 288 pages. $47.50. A sumptuous catalogue of equipment and artifacts compiled by a master collector.

THE INVENTED EYE:
MASTERPIECES OF PHOTOGRAPHY, 1839-1914
By Edward Lucie-Smith. Paddington Press Ltd/Two Continents Publishing Group, New York. 256 pages. $16.95. Photography's first 75 years by an English art critic.

THE MAGIC IMAGE: THE GENIUS OF PHOTOGRAPHY FROM 1839 TO THE PRESENT
By Cecil Beaton and Gail Buckland. Little, Brown & Company, Boston. 304 pages. $19.95. An English master's gallery of the major contributors to the evolution of photography.

Technical

THE CRAFT OF PHOTOGRAPHY
By David Vestal. Harper & Row, Publishers, New York. 364 pages. $12.50. An illustrated course in black-and-white photography for both beginners and advanced students.

KODAK PROFESSIONAL PHOTOGUIDE
Eastman Kodak Company, Rochester, N.Y. 40 pages. $8.95. An on-location guide to the right equipment for any given shot.

Roundup/8

Roundup/8

A Crusty Colossus	218
Milestones	228
Miscellany	232

A Crusty Colossus/ WALKER EVANS: *Relic in an Auto Junkyard,* 1974

Roundup

Walker Evans —A Crusty Colossus

Whenever the late documentary master raised his camera — or his voice — he always knew exactly what he was going to say

by Loudon Wainwright

> Loudon Wainwright was a text editor, picture editor and columnist at LIFE for 23 years. He is currently at work on a book about the history of that magazine.

"The motionless camera" author James Agee called the instrument Walker Evans used to take the pictures for *Let Us Now Praise Famous Men,* their extraordinary collaborative work on tenant-farm families during the Depression. And though one would expect no less of such a poet of the precise as Agee, his word "motionless" has qualities of permanence, of images fixed in irretrievable time that make the conventional word "still" seem puny and unfocused. And indeed Evans' pictures of farm wives and children staring at the glass of the lens, or of crude, sign-bedecked country stores and unpainted shanties baking in the Alabama sunlight seem to have been formed in an implacable instrument that revealed the subjects as they really were, not as anyone would wish them to be.

This absolute, blinkless unsentimentality is perhaps the most familiar quality in the work of Walker Evans, who died last year at 71 and was unquestionably one of photography's most important figures. "They were a record of what's what," Evans himself said of the pictures he took of the impoverished 1930s, a period during which he did most of his best-known work; but the same terse definition also applies to the photographs that he took after that great early burst.

"Good photography is unpretentious. One just does it," Evans said in an interview he gave the magazine, *Art in America,* just a few years before his death. "A photographer sees something that speaks to him and he takes it." Thus he simultaneously drove his needle into the self-importance of those round-phrasing mystifiers of the magic of picture-making, and illuminated the cold purity of his own substantial art.

For there is something cold, sometimes even aloof, about Evans' work, although much of his subject matter, especially that involving American poverty, would lead one to believe that his photographs were the expression of a powerful social conscience. Of course, he clearly was sympathetic to human suffering and recalled, in fact, that his photography was in some part "a semiconscious reaction against right thinking and optimism; it was an attack on the establishment." But Walker Evans took pictures that primarily reflected his esthetic judgments, not the leakings of his heart.

To most literate Americans, even Americans moderately interested in photography, Walker Evans is oddly unknown, almost a Mr. What's-his-name at the head table of the arts. While his work is widely and clumsily imitated, it is usually imitated by people who have only some vague recollection of his images, not of his person or his ideas. In a career crossing more than 40 years, his output was not large. Besides the 62 photographs printed in the enlarged edition of *Let Us Now Praise Famous Men,* only three limited collections of his pictures have been published. Much of Walker Evans' best later work, shown on pages 223-227, appeared in FORTUNE between 1945 and 1965,

This portrait of an Alabama sharecropper, one of the best known of Evans' pictures, was taken in the summer of 1936 when he and writer James Agee were documenting the lives of tenant-farm families; eventually their combined work was published—and celebrated— as the book, Let Us Now Praise Famous Men.

where the handsome displays of his photographs offset the modest 300,000 circulation of the magazine at that time. Evans simply was not interested in having his work appear in big picture magazines like LIFE or Look because he felt, correctly, that he would not have the control he wanted over the presentation of his pictures and the words that accompanied them.

Yet this stubborn man who for years would not use color film, who ridiculed technique ("This technical perfection is the fault of many photographers. They take perfect pictures with no content.") and whose vanity was occasionally laced with contempt ("To be an interesting photographer, one must have an interesting mind.") clearly stood apart. His genius stood unchallenged by critics, who were stunned at the blunt simplicity of his photographs. And the genius was acknowledged early on, in the 1930s; Evans did not get gray and cranky waiting for professional recognition.

"The power of Evans' work," wrote the critic Lincoln Kirstein, "lies in the fact that he so details the effect of circumstances on familiar specimens that the single face, the single house, the single street strikes with the force of overwhelming numbers, the terrible cumulative force of thousands of faces, houses and streets." Perhaps, too, the pictures, like leaves of some raw calendar of film he passed beneath his shutter, draw us into a time and an experience we may have never known, yet must now see as the utter truth.

Walker Evans was born in Saint Louis in 1903, and was raised in a Chicago suburb by his mother after his parents had separated. A child of comfortable economic circumstances, he was sent back East to boarding school and college. But he left Williams College after one year and in the mid-20s went to Paris. There he attended some classes at the Sorbonne and enjoyed himself in a bohemian existence that was a great relief from the stuffy materialism of the American life he'd rejected.

During this period, he bought a simple, fixed-lens Kodak camera and began taking pictures as an amateur. He was much impressed with the work of Eugène Atget, particularly by his photographs of Paris. "But then I suppose," Evans recalled, "I thought photographing was a minor thing to be doing. And I guess I thought I ought to be writing. But in writing I felt blocked—mostly by high standards. I'd done a lot of reading, and I knew what writing was."

Back in the United States in the late '20s, Evans decided to devote his life to photography, though his interest in writing remained strong—much later he wrote with real, evocative skill in the text accompanying the picture portfolios he did for FORTUNE. But he became absorbed in photography, so absorbed that at times he thought he was going mad, the symptoms possibly heightened by the fact that for 18 months he held a night job to support himself and wasn't getting enough sleep.

The French experience stayed with him, and he spoke often of the in-

Roundup / Walker Evans

fluences on his attitudes of the work of Flaubert and Baudelaire. "Flaubert's realism and his naturalism both," were characteristics that had a great effect on Evans. He also admired "the nonappearance of author, the nonsubjectivity. That is literally applicable to the way I want to use a camera and do. But, spiritually, it is Baudelaire who is *the* influence on me." And indeed one can feel, looking at Evans' abandoned cars or into the dead-calm eyes of the children he photographed in the South, the Baudelaire whom Stephen Spender has called "the Fisher King of the modern Waste Land," the poet who struggles "in his own imagination to adapt the vision of the past to the heroism, boredom and squalor of modern life."

Evans did not pursue the trappings of squalor in his private life. In fact, he was entirely fond of many of the finer things—a pair of good English shoes, an excellent wine, a Jaguar automobile with soft leather seats. Just as his somber vision did not diminish his taste, it did not increase his humility, either, and his acid arrogance was displayed rather early in his career. He felt snubbed, for example, in an introductory encounter with the great photographer Alfred Stieglitz, whom Evans held in awed regard. He took Stieglitz's alleged indifference toward him hard and held it firmly against his erstwhile hero referring to him on one occasion as "a great old fiddler and lace-maker . . . pure and esthetic, with money behind him."

Walker Evans *did* admire Mathew Brady along with Eugène Atget, but his enthusiasm for most highly regarded photographers was, to understate the case, limited. At one time, in a sort of roundhouse aimed at virtually the whole profession, he said, "The main thing is whether you have something original, something all your own to say. And I'm afraid the only photographers I can think of who do *invent,* who create their own way for themselves are myself, Henri [Cartier-Bresson] and Helen Leavitt. As for the rest, they're all imitating somebody."

Yet when it came to describing what he was doing, what artistic ends he sought to achieve, he had a certain real modesty. "I was very lucky," he told one interviewer. "I just came upon my true line without going down bypaths or blind alleys or dead ends.

"And I can't tell you how I go about my work either," he emphasized to another. "I speak from very unhappy experience. I used to analyze it, to try to figure out exactly what I was doing all the time, and that inhibited me, terribly, until I found out that I didn't have to go through all that at all. My work is like making love, if you'll forgive me. It has to spring from the moment, from what I feel at the moment. That's all."

Yet, on occasion, he tried to express it better than that, to his friends, and as a teacher at Yale in the last years of his life. He especially reached out in his explanations for a description of transcendence, for a quality that was a

A 1938 Evans' collection, entitled "American Photographs," was filled with powerful, unadorned documentary pictures like the three shown here: a couple at Coney Island (below), a relic from a destroyed building (below, right), and cars parked like toys on a glistening, empty street of rainy Saratoga Springs, New York.

level beyond the obvious. "You're trying for something," he said, "and if it's wrong, you know later on. But first you get it on the film, you *garner it in.* [If] it's transcendent, you feel it. It's there, the vanished transcendent, an instance of chance, action and fortuity. It's there, and you can't unfeel it."

It made him angry if anyone confused the tone of his work with nostalgia. He deplored nostalgia and its cheap tugs. "It's not supposed to bring tears to your eyes," he said of one subject, but with a vehemence applicable to all of his work. "It is supposed to make you feel that that is the way it was."

Upon retirement from Yale in 1972, he was named a professor emeritus, and the moss-hung title must have given a laugh now and then to that disdainful rebel of earlier days. Of course, he liked the young ("God bless them. They've been lied to so often.") and he liked the recognition ("I haven't strived for it, but it makes me feel that justice does exist."). Still, he had private ways of viewing himself that were as merciless as the ways he looked at other subjects of his fierce attention. Asked about self-portraits, he said: "I've taken some pictures of myself, but don't like to have other persons see them. I think they're not me. Do we know what we look like? Not really."

And looking at himself near the end—and perhaps before that, too—Evans must have found it at least somewhat hard to accept the fact that the reputation so awe-inspiring to his students and other admirers was based on work he'd done 30 and 40 years before. They were interested in his early '30s pictures of the workers and cars and billboards and buildings he'd shot, during the Depression. Thus he became known as the documenter without peer of a single era in the American past, and it was almost overlooked that his talent was of even greater size, and covered a broader span of time.

The writing he did for his own picture essays at FORTUNE must have given him solid pleasure. For whatever he said about his writing, Evans was good at it. In an introductory essay in *Let Us Now Praise Famous Men,* he wrote of James Agee that he "worked in what looked like a rush and a rage," and that he "did a lot of talking in the air. He seemed to model, fight and stroke his phrases as he talked." In a FORTUNE essay on Chicago he wrote: "A Prairie Avenue mansion is ripped down to save taxes, but its marble gateposts and vine-shrouded iron fence are left leaning into the future."

There it is—that Baudelairean view again, that perspective of life in ruins and ruins in life that drove this wry and tough man who was one of the finest artists of his time. He found it everywhere. "But in a week," Walker Evans wrote for a picture essay on the demolition of buildings, "this will just be a flat open space strewn with ground-leavings—two thirds of a plaster acanthus, a serpent of electric wire from 1903, one ormolu table leg, a chipped porcelain plaque marked EXIT." These words serve as a description, not only of a single assignment but of the man's extraordinary vision of life.

Roundup/**Walker Evans**

The Evans No One Remembers

Most people know the Walker Evans who was a photographer of Southern farms. It has been almost forgotten that from 1945 to 1965 Evans worked on the staff of FORTUNE magazine where he turned out some 40 essays containing a rich lode of spare, often stark, perceptions of the kind that had won him a worldwide reputation as a documentary photographer in the 1930s.

The editors who gave him his first assignments at FORTUNE were not certain just how his powerful images and very definite point of view might fit into the magazine's format. However, his pictures were so striking that they soon began tailoring the magazine's pages to suit them. And shortly they stopped telling him what to do altogether.

"He'd go off for months at a time," reminisced a FORTUNE staff member recently, "just shooting whatever struck him." Evans took many of his FORTUNE pictures in color, a departure from his familiar black-and-white photography. He began writing the text and captions, too; here and on the following pages is a selection of these words and pictures from the FORTUNE years.

> "Poland Spring House was designed with the prodigality of a Wagner opera and the verve of a Sousa march. It is probably the most exuberant resort hotel building in the world. Certainly few others approach its architectural fanfare and crash of cymbals. In association of forms, Poland Spring manages to bring you Carcassonne and Italian Baroque; Caesar Augustus, Pericles, and Chester A. Arthur all at once."

Poland Spring House, Poland Spring, Maine, 1949

Roundup/**Walker Evans**

"In Roomette 6, Car 287, the light has not yet been switched on. For an hour the train has swayed and rattled across the land. Now if ever, in this place and in this mood, the traveler can abandon himself to the rich pastime of window-gazing. Along the paths of railroads, the country is in semi-undress. You can see some of the anatomy of its living: a back yard with its citizens poking into a rumble seat for a trusted toolbox; an intent group of boys locked in a sandlot ball game; a fading factory wall; a lone child with a cart."

New Jersey Factory Town, Photographed from a Moving Train, 1950

"There never was anything quite like those pounding, hissing, snorting, screeching beasts. Their day is almost done. And when they are finally still, men will think over and talk over just what their great appeal was. It may come down to this: the steam locomotive embodied the joy of purposeful uproar."

Drivers of a Steam Locomotive on a Track near Roanoke, Virginia, 1958

Roundup/**Walker Evans**

"Among low-priced, factory-produced goods, none is so appealing to the senses as the ordinary hand tool. Aside from their function —though they are exclusively wedded to function—each of these tools lures the eye to follow its curves and angles, and invites the hand to test its balance."

"They speak with their eyes. People out of work are not given to talking much about the one thing on their minds. You only sense, by indirection, degrees of anger, shades of humiliation, and echoes of fear. The people shown here were all informed, voluntary (and generous) participants in the portraiture. They are not the hundred neediest cases—or the million. Mostly they are just laid-off citizens."

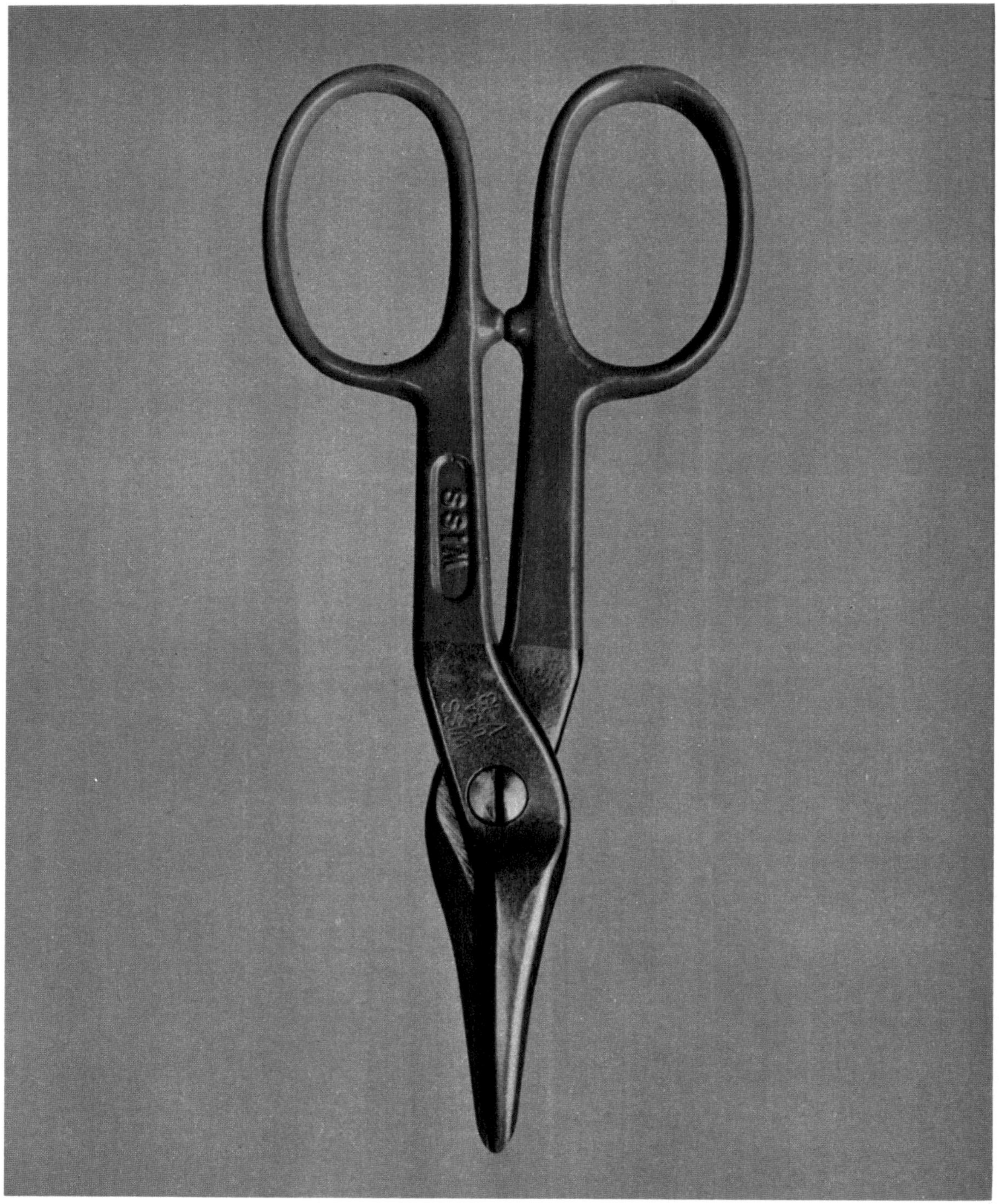

Tin Snips, 1955

An Unemployed Worker, 1961

Roundup

Milestones

Charles Hoff 1905-1975

The man who made one of the most famous news photographs of all time—the German zeppelin *Hindenburg* belching flames only moments after it had exploded *(below)*—died at 70 after a distinguished 41-year career as a staff photographer for New York City tabloids. Charles Hoff was on a routine assignment to cover the landing of the dirigible at Lakehurst, New Jersey, on May 6, 1937, when, already at its mooring mast, the airship suddenly blew up and destroyed itself in just 32 seconds. "I only tried to keep my hands from trembling as I slid plates into the camera," recalled Hoff, who was known among his colleagues for his swift and steady reflexes.

During his four decades of newspaper work, Hoff covered all the standard news beats, from police stations to car accidents and ticker-tape parades. In his later years he became one of the first news photographers to make extensive use of strobe lights at sports events. Sharp images of motion frozen at the zenith of action became his specialty and they won him most of the 124 awards he received.

CHARLES HOFF: *The Zeppelin Hindenburg Erupting into Flame*, 1937

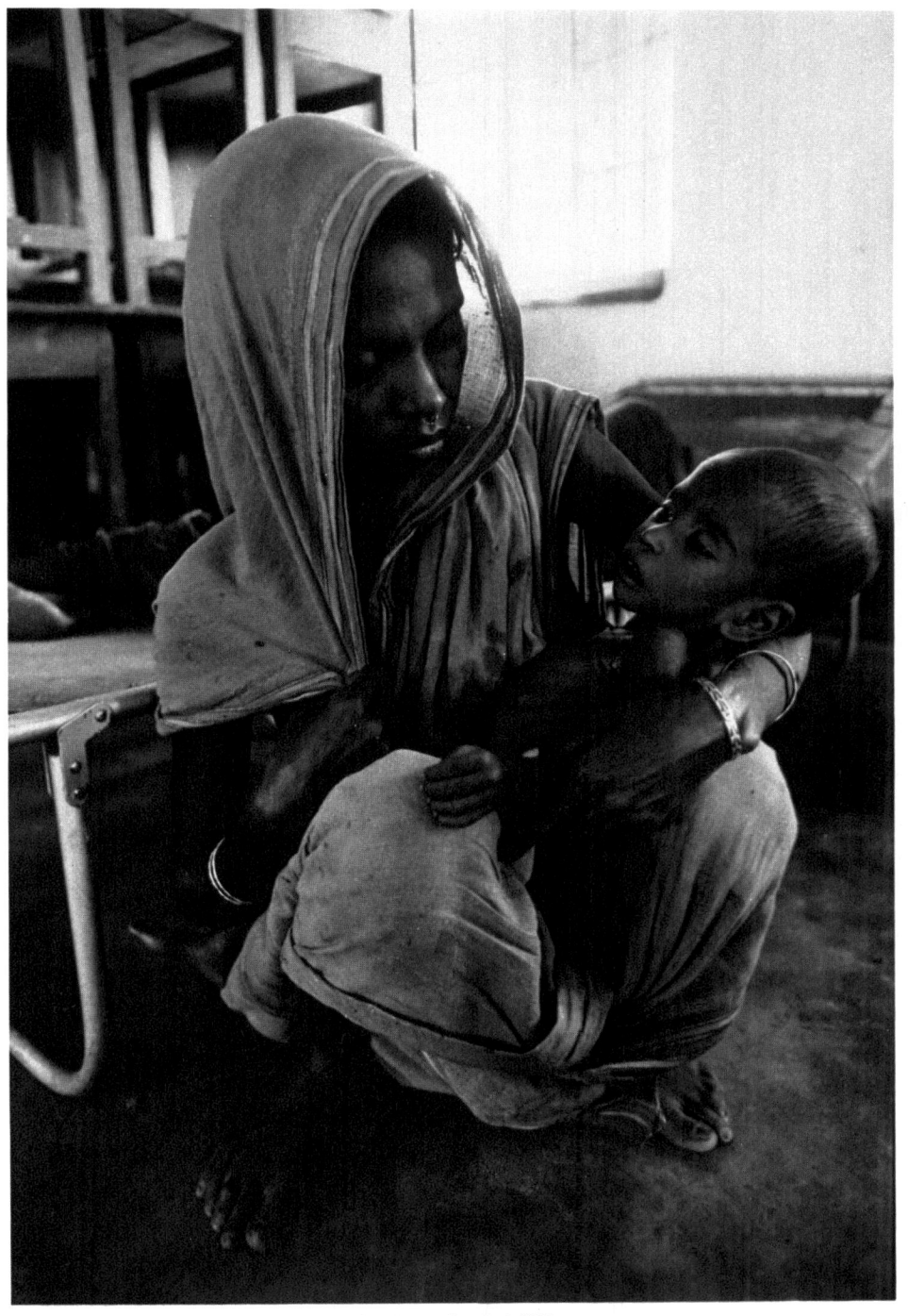

MICHEL LAURENT: *Mother with Dying Infant in a Dacca Hospital,* 1974

Michel Laurent 1946-1975

Just two days before the fall of Saigon, on April 28, 1975, Pulitzer prize-winning photographer Michel Laurent became the 39th and last newsman known to have died in the 30-year Indochina war. Laurent was covering maneuvers by some South Vietnamese militia when they were ambushed by Communist troops. Dodging bullets, Laurent had managed to reach his jeep when he saw that a fellow French newsman, Christian Hoche, had been wounded and was stranded between the two opposing forces. Laurent ran back to try to rescue Hoche and, caught in a crossfire, was killed instantly. Hoche survived.

Laurent was 28 when he died, but he had had an active and varied career during his 12 years as a photojournalist. A native of Paris, he covered the French presidential campaigns, first for the Associated Press and later for the Paris-based Gamma photo agency. In war, he photographed not only in Vietnam but in Jordan, Nigeria, Israel, Cyprus and Bangladesh; in l972 he won the Pulitzer prize for a photo essay on the Bangladesh struggle.

Throughout his career he was always interested in—and known for his images of—the victims of floods and famines as well as war. Typical of his sympathetic portrayal of disaster's effects is the poignant picture at left of a stoic Bengali mother, cradling her starving infant while waiting for help in a Dacca hospital.

Roundup/**Milestones**

JOHN VACHON: *Riding the Ranch in Winter,* 1938

John Vachon 1914-1975
John Vachon, whose lyric essays for *Look* magazine reflected his deep concern for the vanishing America of family farms and small towns, died in April.

"I am a photographer by pure accident," recalled Vachon, who had planned for a career as a writer. Forced to leave graduate school by the Depression, he obtained a stopgap job as a messenger and photo cataloguer for Roy Stryker *(page 231)* at the Farm Security Administration. As he stamped and filed the prints of Walker Evans, Dorothea Lange and others, Vachon became fascinated by photography, borrowed a Leica, and so impressed Stryker with his pictures that he was made a photographer.

On his first long assignment for the FSA, Vachon took the picture above of a horseman and his dog on a winter's day in the Dakota Great Plains. He developed a lifelong love for "that land of vast space and wild blowing snow," returning almost annually to photograph it. But Vachon was not merely a one-theme photographer: he also photographed Latin American oil workers, war-ravaged Poland, family life in Ireland, and even fashion.

Herbert List 1903-1975

Herbert List, one of Germany's best-known photojournalists, died in Munich in April. Until his midthirties, List was a coffee importer and practiced photography only as an amateur. But he left Germany in 1936 after the Nazis took over. Arriving in London without money, List launched himself on a new—and extremely successful—career as a photographer.

List quickly gained a reputation for portraits, still lifes, landscapes and travel essays. After the Second World War his resounding success as a photographer enabled him to "travel a lot and live quite well." His travels resulted in five books—on Greece, Africa, Mexico, the Caribbean and Italy.

Most of List's work appeared, internationally, in picture magazines: France's *Verve,* the Swiss publication *Du,* the British *Picture Post,* Italy's *Epoca* and, in America, *LIFE* and *Look.* Another American magazine, *Vogue,* commissioned and published most of his famous portraits of artists and writers.

Wynn Bullock 1902-1975

At his death Wynn Bullock was one of the acknowledged masters of American nature photography. He started out in life, however, to become a concert tenor. While on a European concert tour in 1928, he visited the Louvre in Paris where he saw the landscape paintings of the French Impressionists. He was so moved by their use of light that he decided to abandon his promising singing career and instead, to express himself visually—not as a painter but as a photographer.

The focal point for his talents, in fact for his life, was the rugged Pacific coast around his adopted home town of Monterey, California. Here he took his most famous pictures —undulating beaches with rocky palisades, pale nudes in quiet ferny woods, and close-ups of the swirling textures of weathered wood.

Like his close friend and fellow photographer, Edward Weston, Bullock was a consummate craftsman. To render details with pristine clarity, he used an 8 × 10-inch view camera and made same-size contact prints directly from the negative. His skill is strikingly evident in his flawless original prints, which are filled with nuances of tone—and especially with contrasts of light.

For Bullock, light was the all-important ingredient. "Light," he once commented, "is a physical entity that offers photography the plasticity that sound offers to music and paint offers to painting."

Roy Stryker 1891-1975

Roy Stryker—the man who both inspired and directed the photographers now famed for their documentation of the Great Depression —died only a few months after two of the most notable photographers he had guided: John Vachon *(page 230)* and Walker Evans *(page 218).* As director of the Historical Section of the Farm Security Administration from 1935 to 1942, Stryker and his photographers created a monumental archive of 150,000 photographs that recorded virtually every aspect of American life.

Among Stryker's FSA photographers were Dorothea Lange, Ben Shahn, Carl Mydans, Russell Lee and Arthur Rothstein. They spread out to cover urban as well as rural America, but their best-known pictures are the ones depicting the plight of sharecroppers, coal miners and dust-bowl victims; these scenes helped arouse public and congressional support for New Deal social legislation.

Stryker was not a photographer. He had been a cowboy, soldier, and economics instructor, but at the FSA—and later, on other documentary projects—he developed a close relationship with his photographers, influencing their art, and sometimes even their lives. Describing his FSA days, he recalled: "I was one-half editor, one-half papa, one-half hell raiser, one-half purchasing agent, and occasionally psychoanalyst without portfolio."

Roundup

Miscellany

Rubbing Shoulders with Yesterday

Vienna had a problem: construction of the Austrian capital's first subway had turned a busy shopping street, the Graben, into an eyesore. And the city fathers needed some way to hide the ugly excavation gash from a public sensitive to beauty. The solution that they found proved a unique visual surprise.

Life-sized enlargements of turn-of-the-century photographs—showing top-hatted Viennese gentlemen, nannies in ruffled skirts and portly officers from the Austrian general staff—were mounted on the fences that surround the subway trench. The enlarged photographs, 50 in all, were selected from a book called *The Good Old Times,* which was compiled by a Viennese photographer and collector of old prints, Franz Hubmann. The stretch of wall shown at right stands near the spot on the Graben where the 1908 photograph of the two Austrian generals had been taken originally.

Viennese pedestrians were so enchanted with the walls that the city plans to apply the photo-wall solution to future construction sites. Collector Hubmann was especially pleased by the daily exposure of his pictures, and remarked, "I don't think any one has ever had as large a showroom and as varied a public for his treasures."

Street-side Photo-watchers on Vienna's Graben

The Barn That Became the Fox Talbot Photography Museum

The Mezzanine (top) and Main Floor of the Museum

A Barn for Photography

On the 27th of June, 1975, modern photography came home. On that day Britain's National Trust finished turning a 16th Century stone barn into the only museum in England devoted entirely to photography. The barn stands near the entrance to Lacock Abbey, the ancestral estate of the 19th Century photography pioneer William Henry Fox Talbot, where, in 1840, Talbot created the calotype—a process that allowed photographers to produce multiple positive prints from a single negative. It is on the calotype process that modern photography is based.

The museum's designers left the exterior of the barn untouched, but they modified the interior by adding air conditioning, humidifiers, modern lighting, and a mezzanine constructed of oak and elm.

The mezzanine is given over to exhibitions of both historical and contemporary photographic work. A small audio-visual theater at one end of the mezzanine shows slides of Fox Talbot's life, while an office on the opposite end is used for visiting researchers. The ground floor houses an invaluable collection of Fox Talbot prints, biographical material and memorabilia as well as a shop that carries books on early photography.

The Abbey and its grounds still retain the same serene beauty that they had when Fox Talbot used them as the background for many of his notable pictures. In fact, the striking architecture and sense of history at Lacock Abbey induced one of its early visitors to murmur, "No wonder photography was invented here; it had to be."

Clicking at Yashica

Once a healthy giant of Japan's camera industry, the Tokyo-based Yashica, Inc. had fallen critically ill by the early 1970s. The recession hurt sales; a director was arrested for embezzlement; and two top men, when they heard rumors that their plant was to be closed, tried (and failed) to commit hara-kiri.

Then, in 1975, Yashica's fortunes took a dramatic turn. A prime reason was the hard-line approach of its new president, Shiro Kaneko, who slashed the company's payroll, closed a second, unprofitable plant, and started to assemble cameras—of their lower and middle price range —in Hong Kong, where labor costs are one fourth those of Japan.

Kaneko hopes that his efforts will erase Yashica's $6,000,000 deficit within a few years.

Roundup/**Miscellany**

Free Forum for Journalists

On August 13, 1975, the first truly pictorial newspaper in the United States was launched. Called San Francisco News and made up of single photos and essays with only the barest captions, it had a press run of 15,000 copies monthly.

The News was the counterculture brainchild of an eclectic mix of journalists and news photographers who had worked for such establishment papers as the New York Daily News and the San Francisco Chronicle. Their aims were simple: to present, in photographs, aspects of San Francisco life that, according to one editor, "would not get lost in a lot of type."

To finance publication and distribution, the News' staff of 25 worked without salary and depended on advertising, mainly from local photography shops.

The News quickly became well enough known in San Francisco to attract giveaway photography from 100 photographers. Much encouraged, the editors made plans for a spin-off: a series of books dealing with life in the Bay City.

Experiment in Arizona

In May 1975, the University of Arizona in Tucson opened its Center for Creative Photography and introduced a radical concept for acquiring archival material. The curators, armed with funds of $400,000, bought ultimate rights to the negatives, as well as selected work prints, notebooks, journals and letters produced by five major American photographers—Ansel Adams, Wynn Bullock, Harry Callahan, Aaron Siskind and Frederick Sommer.

The photographers retain full use of their materials while they are alive. The contracts provide for up to 10-year payouts, ensuring regular income for the artists, and encouraging them to produce a steady supply of work for the Center.

The Staff of the San Francisco News

A Fake Leica MP Camera

Leica Look-Alike

Collectors of rare Leica cameras received a rude jolt in 1975. *The Wall Street Journal* reported that some of the examples of one of their most sought-after specimens—the Leica MP—are fakes.

Since Leica introduced its first camera in 1925, the jewel-like instruments have been collected by enthusiasts whose ambition to own every Leica variant (some 200 in all) has earned them the name "Leicamaniacs." But, as the collectors discovered to their chagrin, their craze for these precision cameras also spawned a clever crook.

The Leica MP, a model designed in the 1950s for press photographers, was fetching prices up to $2,400. It was actually a modified Leica M2, a model that sells for around $300. Apparently a camera repairman stole top plates from Leica's factory in Wetzlar, West Germany. He screwed the MP top plate onto an M2 body and, with the addition of a few more parts, produced an authentic-looking MP.

While the phantom fraudsman's exploits raised the hackles of serious Leica collectors, they also produced a new form of Leicamania: there were reports of at least three collectors who had knowingly purchased the bogus MPs just so they could claim they owned what may someday prove to be one of the rarest Leicas of all.

A Bull Market for Photography

In spite of the economic recession, 1975 saw photography move strongly for the first time into the big money world of the international art galleries. Marlborough Gallery Inc, the world's largest dealer in contemporary art, marked its inaugural exhibit of photographic prints with a celebrity-strewn spectacular at its Manhattan-based headquarters.

And New York City dealer Leo Castelli, the man who discovered and merchandized Pop Art, added a select group of young photographers to his fashionable stable of avant-garde artists. Castelli's prestigious gallery began to handle photographic works by Ralph Gibson, Robert Adams and John Gossage. At prices of $175 to $500 per print, trading, according to Castelli, was "immensely active."

The most ambitious—and surely the most talked about—photo art event of the trend-setting 1975 season was the September opening of fashion photographer and portraitist Richard Avedon's one-man exhibit at Marlborough. Avedon was represented by 106 of his photographs—the majority of them unvarnished studies of celebrities—that range from 6-by-6-inch prints to one 8-by-35-foot work showing American advisers in Vietnam and selling for $20,000.

On the opening night, some 3,000 potential purchasers, art world celebrities, photo groupies and movie stars packed the gallery. As swarms of photographers snapped away, one curious but undazzled woman, who finally gave up trying to get a clear look at Avedon's photographs amid the mobs of photographers, commented, "This evening is a parody of itself!"

Avedon's Panorama of Viet Nam Advisers

Roundup/**Miscellany**

Honors for a Camera-shy Genius

For the first time, an English university gave an honorary doctorate to a photographer. That the university was England's prestigious Oxford, and that the recipient was Henri Cartier-Bresson, 67—whom many consider the greatest living photographer—made the event especially memorable.

Although Cartier-Bresson is most celebrated for a style of photography that reveals the human subject in all its pathos, strength and humor, the photographer himself is camera shy. As he strode through Oxford's medieval streets on the way to the investiture ceremony, he covered his face with his mortarboard. The odd behavior was no mere show of false modesty. Cartier-Bresson believes that if he becomes a familiar public figure, the reactions of his subjects will be less natural. So deep is this concern for visual anonymity that the photographer almost turned down Oxford's degree. Cartier-Bresson has twice refused his native country's highest decoration, the French *Légion d' honneur.* But "on behalf of photography," he made an exception for Oxford.

Once he had agreed to accept the honor he could not resist trying to get the kind of candid photographs that have made him famous, and he carried his Leica with him. But Oxford regulations forbid photography during the ceremonies, so the master came away with no pictures—if not exactly empty-handed.

A Shy Cartier-Bresson at Oxford

Bibliography

General
Editors of TIME-LIFE BOOKS, *Life Library of Photography.* TIME-LIFE BOOKS, 1970-1972.
Focal Press, *The Focal Encyclopedia of Photography.* Focal Press, London, 1965.
Friedman, Joseph S., *History of Color Photography.* The American Photographic Publishing Company, 1944.
Gernsheim, Helmut, *Creative Photography.* Faber & Faber, London, 1962.
Gernsheim, Helmut and Alison, *The History of Photography from the Camera Obscura to the Beginning of the Modern Era.* McGraw-Hill, 1969.
Mertens, Lawrence E., *In-Water Photography.* Wiley-Interscience, 1970.
Newhall, Beaumont, *The History of Photography.* The Museum of Modern Art, 1964.

Special Essays
Agee, James, and Walker Evans, *Let Us Now Praise Famous Men.* Houghton-Mifflin Company, 1941.
Armitage, Merle, *Henrietta Shore.* E. Weyhe, Inc., 1933.
Beaton, Cecil, and Gail Buckland, *The Magic Image.* Little, Brown & Company, 1975.
Bullock, Wynn, *Wynn Bullock.* Scrimshaw Press, 1971.
Caulfield, H. J. and Sun Lu, *The Applications of Holography.* John Wiley & Sons, Inc., 1970.
Constantine, Mildred, *Tina Modotti: A Fragile Life.* Paddington Press Ltd., 1975.
Dakin, Henry S., *High-Voltage Photography.* H. S. Dakin, 1974.
De Cock, Liliane, ed., *Wynn Bullock/Photography: A Way of Life.* Morgan & Morgan, Inc., 1973.
Evans, Walker, *Walker Evans.* The Museum of Modern Art, 1971.
Frankel, Tobia, *The Russian Artist.* The Macmillan Company, 1972.
Good, Michael, et al., *Through Our Eyes.* The Lorain Journal, 1974.
History of the Second World War. BPC Publishing Ltd., London, 1974.
Hohenberg, John, *The Pulitzer Prizes.* Columbia University Press, 1974.
Hubmann, Franz, *Die Gute Alte Zeit* (The Good Old Times). St. Peter, Salzburg, 1975.
Katz, Leslie, "An Interview with Walker Evans," *Art in America,* March-April 1971.
Kron, Joan, "Copping a Feel at Vogue," *New York,* May 26, 1975.
Kuwahara, Kineo, *Tokyo Showa Juichinen* (Tokyo, 1936) Shobunsha, Tokyo, 1974.
Lehmann, Matt, *Holography: Technique and Practice.* Focal Press, London, 1970.
Levin, Phyllis Lee, *The Wheels of Fashion.* Doubleday & Company, 1965.
McGraw-Hill Encyclopedia of Russia and the Soviet Union. McGraw-Hill, 1961.
Maddow, Ben, *Edward Weston: Fifty Years.* Aperture, Inc., 1973.
"Venus Beheaded: Weston and His Women," *New York,* February 24, 1975.
Meyer, Armin, "Improvements in the Silver Dye-Bleach Process," *Photographic Science and Engineering,* September 1974.
Mrázková, Daniela, and Vladimír Remeš, *Fotografovali Válku: Sovetská Válecná Reportáz* (They Photographed the War: Soviet War Reportage). Odeon, Prague, 1975.
Ostrander, Sheila, and Lynn Schroeder, *Psychic Discoveries Behind the Iron Curtain.* Prentice-Hall, 1970.
Righini, Mariella, "Les Miroirs de Sarah Moon," *Le Nouvel Observateur,* Paris, Decembre 2, 1974.
Rogliatti, G., *Leica, the First Fifty Years.* Hove Camera Foto Books, Sussex, England, 1975.
Scherman, David E., ed., *Vu par LIFE* (The Best of LIFE). TIME-LIFE International (Nederland) B.V., Amsterdam, 1974.
Snow, Carmel, with Mary Louise Aswell, *The World of Carmel Snow.* McGraw-Hill, 1962.
Strode, Bill, ed., *Barney Cowherd: Photographer.* The Courier-Journal and The Louisville Times, 1973.
Stroke, George W., *An Introduction to Coherent Optics and Holography.* Academic Press, Inc., 1969.
Tanuma, Takeyoshi, *Musashino.* Asahi Shimbun, Tokyo, 1974.
Tomatsu, Teruaki, *Taiyo No Empitsu* (Pencil of the Sun). Mainichi Shimbun, Tokyo, 1975.
Tsukahara, Takuya, *Shiroi Asobi* (White Play). The Gallery Press, Tokyo, 1973.
Ueda, Shoji, *Izumo.* Mainichi Shimbun, Tokyo, 1974.
Vachon, John, "Tribute to a Man, an Era, an Art," *Harper's,* September 1973.
Werth, Alexander, *Russia at War.* E. P. Dutton & Co., 1964.
Weston, Edward, *The Daybooks of Edward Weston,* Volumes I and II. Aperture, Inc., 1961.

Periodicals
Afterimage. Visual Studies Workshop, Rochester, N.Y.
Aperture. Millerton, N.Y.
Artweek. Oakland, Calif.
The British Journal of Photography. Henry Greenwood, London.
Camera. C. J. Bucher, Lucerne, Switzerland.
Camera Mainichi '75. Mainichi Newspapers, Tokyo.
Camera 35. Popular Publications Inc., New York, N.Y.
Creative Camera. Coo Press, London.
Elle. France Editions et Publications, Paris.
Exchange. Saskatoon, Saskatchewan, Canada.
Image. International Museum of Photography at George Eastman House, Rochester, N.Y.
Marie Claire. Union de Publications et d'Editions Modernes, Paris.
Modern Photography. ABC Leisure Magazines, New York, N.Y.
News Photographer. National Press Photographers Association, New York, N.Y.
Le Nouveau Photocinéma. Publications Photo Cinéma, Paris.
Nova. IPC Magazines Limited, London.
Nueva Lente. Madrid.
Petersen's Photographic. Los Angeles, Calif.
Photographic Science and Engineering. Society of Photographic Scientists and Engineers, Washington, D.C.
Photomethods. Ziff-Davis Publishing, New York, N.Y.
Popular Photography. Ziff-Davis Publishing, New York, N.Y.
The Print Collector's Newsletter. New York, N.Y.
Revue Fotografie. Prague.
SLR Camera. Haymarket Publishing, London.
Smithsonian. Smithsonian Associates, Washington, D.C.
Untitled. Friends of Photography, Carmel, Calif.
The Village Voice. New York, N.Y.
Vogue. Condé Nast Publications, New York, N.Y., Editions Condé Nast, Paris and Condé Nast Publications Ltd., London.
Zoom. La Société Publicness Rédaction, Paris.

Acknowledgments

For her help, the editors are indebted to Diana Edkins, The Museum of Modern Art, New York, N.Y. The editors also thank:
In the Americas—Robert D. Anwyl, Michael Sullivan, *Eastman Kodak Company, Rochester, N.Y.;* Bob Baker, Jon Holmes, *Polaroid Corp., Cambridge, Mass.;* Roger Brandenberg-Horn, Barbara Norfleet Cohn, Cynthia von Thüna, *Carpenter Center for the Visual Arts, Harvard Univ., Cambridge, Mass.;* Maureen Brandreth, *Magnum Photos, New York, N.Y.;* Edna Bullock, *Monterey, Calif.;* Peter C. Bunnell, *Princeton Univ., N.J.;* Joseph Burns, Kenneth Dunkley, Abe Rezny, *New York School of Holography, N.Y.;* Russell Burrows, *New York, N.Y.;* James Chung, *Fuji Photo Film U.S.A., Inc., New York, N.Y.;* Rich Clarkson, *Topeka Capital-Journal, Kansas;* Peter Krause, *Ilford Inc., Paramus, N.J.;* Henry S. Dakin, *San Francisco, Calif.;* Andy Dickerman, *Providence Journal-Bulletin, R.I.;* Sandra Eisert, Kathy Tindall, *The White House, Washington, D.C.;* Embassy of the U.S.S.R., Washington, D.C.; David Falconer, *The Oregonian, Portland, Ore.;* Marina Filicori, *New York, N.Y.;* Rolf Fricke, *Leica Historical Society of America, Rochester, N.Y.;* David Fuess, *Carmel Pine Cone, Calif.;* Imre Gaspar, *Hollywood, Calif.;* Jerry Gay, *The Seattle Times, Wash.;* Rod Goldstein, Maria Goodwin, *National Endowment for the Arts, Washington, D.C.;* Suzanne Goldstein, *Rapho-Photo Researchers, New York, N.Y.;* Wilma Gottlieb, *Santa Monica, Calif.;* Frances Grill, *New York, N.Y.;* David Haberstich, Eugene Ostroff, *Smithsonian Institution, Washington, D.C.;* C. Thomas Hardin, *Louisville Courier-Journal & Times, Ky.;* John Heubacher, Kendall Johnson, Thelma Moss, Barry Tass, *The Neuropsychiatric Institute, UCLA, Los Angeles, Calif.;* Ronald Hoff, *New Hyde Park, N.Y.;* Matthew Isenberg, *Hadlyme, Conn.;* T. H. Jeong, *Lake Forest College, Ill.;* Harold Jones, *Center for Creative Photography, Univ. of Arizona, Tucson;* Tom Keane, *Wilmington News-Journal, Del.;* Fred Knubel, *Columbia Univ., New York, N.Y.;* Robert C. Knudsen, *Annandale, Va.;* James L. Lager, *Closter, N.J.;* Brian Lanker, *Eugene Register-Guard, Ore.;* Robert Lindley, *Buenos Aires;* Norman Lipton, *New York, N.Y.;* Selwyn Lissack, *New York, N.Y.;* Robert R. Littman, *Emily Lowe Gallery, Hofstra Univ., Hempstead, N.Y.;* Harry Lunn, *Lunn Gallery, Washington, D.C.;* Angus McDougall, *School of Journalism, Univ. of Missouri, Columbia;* Courtland T. Milloy Jr., Virginia McSweeney Rodriguez, J. Y. Smith, Bill Snead, Bob Webb, *The Washington Post, D.C.;* Larry Muehling, *General Electric Co., Cleveland, Ohio;* Jiří Nedela, *Fairfield, Conn.;* Beaumont

Newhall, *Albuquerque, N. Mex.;* Lewis M. Phelps, *Roanoke, Va.;* Robert Pledge, *Pledge, New York, N.Y.;* Peggy Poe, *Gilbert Felix and Sharf, Inc., New York, N.Y.;* Charles Ruppmann, *New York Press Photographers' Association, N.Y.;* Vickey Sackett, *Washington, D.C.;* Adelheid Sanford, *New York, N.Y.;* Chuck Scott, *Chicago Tribune, Ill.;* Richard Seachrist, *Minneapolis College of Art and Design, Minn.;* Alexander Semenoick, *New York, N.Y.;* Robert Sperling, *Woodmere, N.Y.;* The staff, *San Francisco News, Calif.;* Burns Stanley, *Dearborn, Mich.;* George W. Stroke, *State Univ. of New York, Stony Brook;* John Szarkowski, *The Museum of Modern Art, New York, N.Y.;* William A. Tiller, *Stanford Univ., Los Altos, Calif.;* Madeline B. Treadwell, *New York, N.Y.;* Susan Tribich, *New York, N.Y.;* Françoise Furstier Vachon, *New York, N.Y.;* Willard Van Dyke, *New York, N.Y.;* Cole Weston, *Carmel, Calif.;* Helen Wright, *New York, N.Y.;* Robert M. Young, *New York, N.Y.*

In Asia and Australia—S. Chang, *Tokyo;* John Dunn, *Melbourne;* Shoichi Imai, *Tokyo;* Shoji Yamagishi, *Camera Mainichi, Tokyo.*

In Europe—Philippe Allemand, *Paris;* Karl Heinz Arndt, Bernd Lohse, *Agfa-Gevaert, Leverkusen, W. Germany;* Adelaïde Barbey, *Secretariat à la Culture, Paris;* George Bardawil, *Le Nouveau Photo Cinéma, Paris;* Henri Cartier-Bresson, *Paris;* Nicole Clarence, Peter Knapp, *Elle, Paris;* Friedrich-W. Cordt, *Leitz, GmbH, Wetzlar, W. Germany;* Vic Coucke, *Europhot, Chalon-sur-Saône;* Sue Davies, *Photographers Gallery, London;* Michel Decron, *Photo, Paris;* James Fraser, Peter Guy, *Gordon Fraser Gallery, London;* Pierre Gassman, *Pictorial Service, Paris;* Jean-Claude Gautrand, *Paris;* L. Fritz Gruber, *Photokina, Cologne;* Mark Haworth-Booth, *Victoria and Albert Museum, London;* Max Heinrich, *German Red Cross, Munich;* Franz Hubmann, *Vienna;* Terry Jones, *Vogue, London;* Jocelyn Kargere, *Vogue, Paris;* Derek Knight, *Royal Photographic Society, London;* Guy Knoché, *Documentation Française, Paris;* Gennadi Koposov, *Union of Soviet Journalists, Moscow;* Willie Landels, *The National Magazine Co., London;* Robert Lassam, *Fox Talbot Museum, Lacock, England;* Jean-Claude Lemagny, *Bibliothèque Nationale, Paris;* Paul-Victor Mackensen, *Deutsche Gesellschaft für Photographie, Cologne;* Daniela Mrázková, *Fotografie, Prague;* Novosti Press Agency, *Moscow;* Michael Regan, *Sports Council, London;* Vladimír Remeš, *Prague;* Ursula Retsky, *Vogue, Paris;* Jean-Maurice Rouquette, *Musées d'Arles, Arles, France;* Georges Tavenas, *Charles Jourdan, Paris.*

Picture Credits
Credits from left to right are separated by semicolons, from top to bottom by dashes.

COVER—Ernst Haas; Ken Kay.

Trends: 11—Sarah Moon, *Vogue,* copyright © 1973 par Les Editions Condé Nast S.A. 13—Anestis Diakopoulos, *The Providence Sunday Journal.* 14—Brian Lanker, *Eugene Register-Guard.* 15—Paul Schuhmann, Louisville *Courier-Journal & Times.* 16—Ovie Carter, *Chicago Tribune.* 17—Bern Ketchum, *The Topeka Daily Capital*—Charles Del Vecchio, *The Washington Post.* 18, 19—Michael Lloyd, Portland *Sunday Oregonian.* 20—Tom Hays, *The Louisville Times.* 21—Jerry Gay, *The Seattle Times.* 22—Linda Wheeler, *The Washington Post.* 23—James Mayo, *Chicago Tribune.* 27—Duane Michals; Deborah Turbeville. 28, 29—Deborah Turbeville, *Vogue,* copyright © 1975 by The Condé Nast Publications Inc.; Deborah Turbeville (2). 30, 31—Deborah Turbeville. 32—Helmut Newton; Helmut Newton, *Vogue,* copyright © 1974 by The Condé Nast Publications Inc. 33, 34, 35—Helmut Newton. 36, 37—David Bailey; Sarah Moon, *Vogue,* copyright © 1973 par Les Editions Condé Nast S.A. 38—Sarah Moon—Sarah Moon, London *Sunday Times.* 39—Sarah Moon, *Elle,*—Sarah Moon for Cacharel—Sarah Moon for Biba. 40—Sarah Moon.

The Major Shows: 43—William Eggleston, courtesy Lunn Gallery/Graphics International Ltd. Pages 45 through 55 courtesy Daniela Mrázková. 45—Ivan Sagin. Anatoli Gavanin. 47—Alexandr Uzian. 48—Mikhail Trakhman. 49—Boris Kudoyarov. 50—Galina Sankova. 51—Georgi Zelma. 52, 53—Viktor Grebnev. 54, 55—Dmitri Baltermants; Yevgeni Khaldey. 57 through 63—William Eggleston, courtesy Lunn Gallery/Graphics International Ltd. 65—From *Tina Modotti: A Fragile Life,* by Mildred Constantine, published by Paddington Press Ltd. and Two Continents Publishing Group, New York. 67—From *Henrietta Shore,* edited by Merle Armitage, published by E. Weyhe, Inc., New York, courtesy Art and Architecture Division, The New York Public Library, Astor, Lenox and Tilden Foundations. 68 through 80—Edward Weston from Rapho/Photo Researchers.

Discoveries: 83—James Henkel; Antonín Nový—Juraj Lipták; Culest Bynum; Yoshiko Yanagisawa. 85—Yoshio Monma; Dagmar Hochova—Colette Urbajtel; Chuck Stefanetti—Neil Kagan; B. Martin. 87 through 91—James Henkel. 93 through 99—Antonín Nový. 101 through 105—Robert C. May. 107 through 111—Shin Yanagisawa. 113 through 118—Juraj Lipták.

Assignments: 121—David Hume Kennerly, The White House. 123—Karl Schumacher, The White House. 125 through 136—David Hume Kennerly, The White House.

The New Technology: 139—Neuropsychiatric Institute, UCLA. 142, 143—Copyright © Steve Borns. 144, 145—Drawings by Nicholas Fasciano. 146, 147—Robert Descharnes; Selwyn Lissack © 1972 ARTnews Associates—Robert Descharnes. 149—Drawing by Nicholas Fasciano. 150, 151—Michael Weiss; Drawings by Nicholas Fasciano. 152, 153—Jack Escaloni. 155, 157—Neuropsychiatric Institute, UCLA. 158—Al Freni, courtesy Eastman Kodak Co.; EPOI. 159—Yashica Inc.; A.I.C. Photo, Inc.; Drawing by Nicholas Fasciano. 160—EPOI; Bell & Howell Co. 161—Document Alpa; Ikelite Underwater Systems; Al Freni, courtesy Spiratone Inc. 162—Al Freni, courtesy General Electric Co.; Ponder & Best, Inc.—Al Freni, courtesy Ponder & Best, Inc. 163—Ponder & Best, Inc.—Nikon, Inc.; Fuji Photo Film USA, Inc. 164—Copal Corp. of America; Polaroid Corp.; Al Freni, courtesy Unicolor Div., Photo Systems Inc.

The Annual Awards: 167—Dave Waterman. 169—Shoji Ueda, from *Izumo,* published by Mainichi Shimbun, Tokyo. 170—Shomei Tomatsu. 171—Kineo Kuwahara, from *Tokyo Showa Juichinen,* published by Shobunsha, Tokyo. 172—Takeyoshi Tanuma, from *Musashino,* published by Asahi Shimbun, Tokyo. 173—Kunio Yamamura. 174—Takuya Tsukahara, from *Shiroi Asobi,* published by The Gallery Press, Tokyo. 175—Pat Crowe, Wilmington (Del.) *News-Journal.* 176—Larry Burrows from TIME-LIFE Picture Agency. 177—Eddie Adams from TIME-LIFE Picture Agency. 178—Matthew Lewis, *The Washington Post.* 179—Vsevolod Tarasevich from Novosti. 180—Deutsches Rotes Kreuz Suchdienst. 181—Jean-Louis Nou. 182—W. Eugene Smith. 183—Jerry Gay, *The Seattle Times.* 184—Ovie Carter, *Chicago Tribune.*

The Year's Books: 187—Ernst Haas. 189 through 195—Josef Koudelka from Magnum. 197, 198, 199—Kishin Shinoyama. 201 through 207—Jerry N. Uelsmann. 209 through 213—Ernst Haas.

Roundup: 217—Walker Evans, copied by Jack Escaloni, courtesy Lunn Gallery. 219—Walker Evans, courtesy Library of Congress. 220—Walker Evans, courtesy Lunn Gallery. 221—Walker Evans, courtesy Library of Congress. 222, 223, 224—Walker Evans for FORTUNE. 225, 226, 227—Walker Evans. 228—New York *Daily News.* 229—Michel Laurent from Gamma/Liaison. 230—John Vachon, courtesy Library of Congress. 232—Harry Weber. 233—Wykamol; Robert Lassam. 234—Im Van. 235—Balthazar Korab, courtesy Burns Stanley; Michael Evans from TIME-LIFE Picture Agency. Original photograph by Richard Avedon. 236—Camera Press.

Index *A numeral in italics indicates a photograph or drawing of the subject mentioned.*

Adams, Ansel, 200
Adams, Eddie, photograph by, *177*
Adams, Robert, 235
Agee, James, *Let Us Now Praise Famous Men,* 218, 219
Agfa-Gevaert: Agfamatic cameras, 158; holographic films, 140
Alpert, Paul, *175*
Alvarez Bravo, Manuel, 84, *85*
Arden, Elizabeth, fashion by, *32*
Asanuma, 35-100mm f/3.5 lens, *163*
Association des Gens d'Image, 176
Auras, photography of. *See* Kirlian photography
Avedon, Richard: fashion photography, 24-25; Marlborough Gallery exhibit, *235*
Awards: Best Press Contributions of the Year, *179;* Kulturpreis, 168, *180;* Magazine Photographer of the Year, 175, *177;* Nendo Sho, 169, *170, 171, 172, 174;* Newspaper Photographer of the Year, 168, *175;* Press Photo of the Year, *184;* Le Prix Nadar, *176;* Le Prix Niepce, *181;* Pulitzer Prize for Feature Photography, *178;* Pulitzer Prize for International Reporting, *184;* Pulitzer Prize for Spot News Photography, 168, *183;* Robert Capa Gold Medal, 168, *182;* Shinjin Sho, *173;* Sports Photographer of the Year, *167*
Azzaro, Loris, fashions by, *35*

Bailey, David, photograph by, *36*
Baltermants, Dmitri, 44; photograph by, *54*
Barnett, Sheridan, fashions by, *38*
Barrie, Scott, fashions by, *30, 33*
Beene, Geoffrey, fashions by, *29*
Bewi Zoom-Spot meter, *164*
Biba, fashion by, *40*
Blass, Bill, fashions by, *29*
Books, new, *187-213,* 214; *A Fine Day* (Shinoyama), *196, 197-199; Gypsies* (Koudelka), 188, *189-195; In America* (Haas), *187,* 208, *209-213; Silver Meditations* (Uelsmann), 200, *201-207*
Bronica EC-TL, *160*
Burrows, Larry, photograph by, *176*
Burrows, Stephen, fashions by, *28-29*
Brady, Mathew, 220
Brandt, Bill, 106
Bullock, Wynn, obituary, 231, 234

Cacharel, fashions by, *40*
Callahan, Harry, 106, 234
Calotype, invention of, 233
Cameras: Agfamatic, 158; Bronica EC-TL, *160;* Contax RTS, *159;* Hanimex XP series, 158; Horizon, 123; Kodak Tele-Instamatic, *158;* Kodak Trimlite, *158;* Leica, *235;* Mamiya M645, *160;* medium format, *160;* Minolta XE series, *159;* Miranda dx-3, *159;* Nikonos III, *161;* 110, *158;* Pentax K series, *159;*
Rebikoff Alpa U-Phot, *161;* Rollei SLX, *160;* Sedic XF series, *158;* 35mm, *159;* underwater, *161;* underwater housings for, *161*
Carpenter Center, Harvard University, 56
Carter, Ovie, 12, photographs by, *16, 184*
Cartier-Bresson, Henri, 220, *236;* awarded honorary degree, 236
Center for Creative Photography (Univ. of Arizona), 234
Chandler, Flora MacDonald, 65, 66
Chicago Tribune, 12; photographs from, *16, 23*
Cibachrome process, 148, 149; characteristics, 149; chemical stages, *150-151;* emulsion layers, *149;* equipment required, *152;* processing steps, *152-153;* professional type, 149
Clarkson, Rich, 12
Color prints from slides. *See* Cibachrome
Contax RTS, *159*
Courier-Journal & Times, Louisville, photograph from, *15*
Courrèges, fashions by, *28-29*
Crowe, Pat, 168; photograph by, *175*

Dali, Salvador, 146, *147;* holograms by, *146-147*
Del Vecchio, Charles, photograph by, *17*
Diakopoulos, Anestis, 12; photograph by, *13*
Discoveries, 84, *85;* James Henkel, *83, 86;* Juraj Lipták, *83,* 112; Robert May, *83,* 100; nominees, 86; Antonín Nový, *83,* 92; Shin Yanagisawa, *83,* 106
Dyes: azo, 149; bleaching, 148, *151;* light absorption, 149, *150, 151*

Eastman Kodak: holographic films, 140; 110 cameras, *158*
Eggleston, William, 56; photographs by, *43, 57-63*
Electronic Flash, Vivitar Model 283, *162*
Elle, 25
Enlarger focusing aid, *164*
Estée Lauder, fashion by, *36-37*
Eugene Register Guard, 12; photograph from, *14*
Evans, Walker, 106, 218-221, 222; "American Photographs," 220-221; early photography, 219; early life, 219; and Farm Security Administration, 231; FORTUNE essays, 218, 219, 221, *222-227; Let Us Now Praise Famous Men,* 218, 219; opinions, 220-221; quoted, 218, 219, 220, 221
Exposure meters: Bewi Zoom-Spot, *164;* Sekonic L-428, *164;* silicon cell, 164

Farm Security Administration photographers, 231; and Roy Stryker, 230, 231; and John Vachon, 230. *See also* Evans, Walker
Farova, Anna, 84, *85*
Fashion photography: evolution, 24-25; new modes, 11, 24, 25-26, 27-40
Film: holographic, 140, 144; Polacolor 2, *164*
Flash equipment: FlipFlash, *cover,* 4, *162;* Vivitar Model 283, *162*
FlipFlash, *cover,* 4, *162*
Ford, Betty, 123, *131,* 136
Ford, Gerald, *121, 123, 125, 126, 127, 129, 130, 132-133, 136;* and David Hume Kennerly, 122-124
Ford, Susan, *131*
FORTUNE: and Walker Evans, 218, 219, 221, 222; photographs from, *222-227*
Fotografie, 44
Fox Talbot Photography Museum, 233
Frank, Robert, 106
Fuji, EBC Fujinon SF 85mm F/4 lens, *163*

Gabor, Dennis, 146
Galleries, photography in: Castelli, *235;* Marlborough, *235*
Garanin, Anatoli, 46; photograph by, *46*
Gaspar, Bela, 148, 149; Gasparcolor, 148
Gay, Jerry, 12, 168; photographs by, *21, 183*
General Electric, FlipFlash, *cover,* 4, *162*
Gibson, Ralph, 235
Goedecke Ewa-Marine, *161*
Gossage, John, 235
Grebnev, Viktor, photograph by, *52-53*

Haas, Ernst, 208; *In America, cover,* 4, *187,* 208, *209-213*
Hanimex XP cameras, 158
Hays, Tom, photograph by, *20*
Henkel, James, *83,* 86; photographs by, *87-91*
Hindenburg, explosion of, 12, *228*
Hoche, Christian, 229
Hoff, Charles: obituary, *228;* photograph by, *228*
Holograms, *142-143, 146-147;* interference pattern of, *142;* making transmission type, 143, 144, *145;* types, 143; viewing, 140, 142, 143
Holography, 140-143, *144-145;* difficulties, 142-143, 144; exhibits, 140, 146; home equipment for, 140-141, 142-143, *144-145;* image recording, 141-142; optical components, *144;* optical table, 143, 144, *145;* schools, 140
House of Soviet Science and Culture (Prague), 44
Hubman, Franz: photo wall, *232; The Good Old Times,* 232

Ikelite Underwater Systems, SX-70 housing, *161*
International Center for Photography (New York), 140
International Kirlian Research Associates, 154

Japan Photography Society, 169
Jones, Harold, 84, *85*

Kaneko, Shiro, 233
Kazakh State University (Alma-Ata, USSR), Kirlian photography at, 156
Kennerly, David Hume, 122, *123,* 124; photographs by, *121, 125-136*
Ketchum, Bern, 17; photograph by, *16*
Khaldez, Yevgeni, photograph by, *54-55*
Khanh, Emmanuelle, fashions by, *34*
Kirlian, Semyon and Valentina, 154, 155
Kirlian photography, 154-156; Creeping Charley phenomenon, 154, *155,* 156; criticism of, 155-156; history, 155; implications, 156; International Kirlian Research Associates, 154; photographs, *139, 155, 157;* technique, 154
Kirstein, Lincoln, quoted on Walker Evans, 219
Kissinger, Henry, *129, 134, 135*
Knoedler & Company, M., 140
Kodak. *See* Eastman Kodak
Koudelka, Josef, 92, 188; *Gypsies,* 188, *189-195*
Kudoyarov, Boris, photograph by, *49*
Kuwahara, Kineo, photograph by, 168, *171*

Lacock Abbey, 233
Lagerfeld, Karl, fashions by, *27, 39*
Lancaster, fashion by, *36-37*
Lanker, Brian, 12; photograph by, *14*
Lasers and holography, 141, 143, *145*
Laurent, Michel, obituary, *229;* photograph by, *229*
Leavitt, Helen, 220
Leica, counterfeit, *235*
Lenses: Asanuma 35-105mm f/3.5, *163;* EBC Fujinon SF 85mm f/4, *163;* Micro-Nikkor 105mm f/4, *163;* Nikkor 28-45mm f/4.5, *163;* Rokkor-X 40-80mm f/3.5, *163;* Rokunar 38-90mm f/3.5, *163;* Sigma XQ 39-80mm f/3.5, *163;* Soligor CD 35-105mm f/3.5, *163;* Sun 38-90mm f/3.5, *163;* Vivitar Series 1 35-85mm f/2.8, *163;* Vivitar Series 1 90mm f/2.5, *163*
Lewis, Matthew, photograph by, *178*
Light: coherence, 141; interference, 141, 142
Lipták, Juraj, *83,* 92, 112; photographs by, *113-118*
Lissak, Selwyn, 146; holograms by, *142-143*
List, Herbert, obituary, 231
Lloyd, Michael, photograph by, *18-19*
Louisville Times, The, photograph from, *20*
Lynch, John, *178*

McGee, Silas, *130*
Malcolm, Janet, 69; quoted on Edward Weston, 69
Mamiya M645, *160*
Marie Claire, 25
May, Robert, *83,* 100; photographs by, *101-105*
Mayo, James, 12; photograph by, *23*
Michels, Duane, photograph by, *27*
Minolta: Rokkor-X 40-80mm f/2.8 lens, *163;* XE cameras, 159
Miranda dx-3, *159*
Missoni, fashions by, *34*
Modotti, Tina, *65,* 66, 67; quoted, 67
Moon, Sarah (Marielle Hadengue), 24, 25, *36;* photographs by, *11, 36-40;* quoted, 26, 36
Moss, Thelma, 156
Mrázková, Daniela, 44
Mucha, Alphonse, 92
Muhammad, Elijah, 12, *16*
Muhammad, Wallace, *16*
Muir, Jean, fashions by, *31*
Mullen, William, 185
Munkacsi, Martin, 24
Murray, Joan, 84, *85*
Museum for photography near Lacock Abbey, *233*
Museum of Modern Art, The (New York), 64, 68

National Press Photographers Association, 175
National Trust (Great Britain), *233*
Neuropsychiatric Institute, The (UCLA), Kirlian photographs by, *139, 155,* 156, *157*
News, San Francisco, 234; staff, *234*
Newton, Helmut, 24, 25, 26, *32;* photographs by, *32-35;* quoted, 25
Nguyen Cao Ky, *17*
Nikon, 175; Micro-Nikkor 105mm f/4 lens, *163;* Nikkor 28-45mm f/4.5 lens, *163;* Nikonos III, 161
Nou, Jean-Louis, photograph by, 168, *181*
Nova, 25

Nový, Antonín, 83, 92; photographs by, *93-99*

Okami, Akira, 84, *85*
Orozco, José Clemente, 73
Oxford University, honorary degree to Cartier Bresson, 236

Pentax K series cameras, 159
Photojournalism, new trends in, 12; examples, *13-23*
Pictorial photography, 65
Polaroid: Polacolor 2, *164;* underwater housing for SX-70, 161
Providence Journal-Bulletin, The, 12; photograph from, *13*

Rebikoff-Alpa U-Phot, *161*
Red Cross, German, 168; photo book, *180*
Reger, Janet, fashions by, *38*
Rejlander, O. G., 200
Remeš, Vladimír, 44
Rockefeller, Nelson, *128*
Rokkor-X 40-80mm f/2.8 lens, *163*
Rokunar 38-90mm f/3.5 lens, *163*
Rollei SLX, 160
Rouquette, Jean-Maurice, 84, *85*
Royal Photographic Society (Great Britain), 167

Sadat, Anwar, 122, *135,* 177
Sagin Ivan, photograph by, *45*
Saint Laurent, Yves, fashions by, *30-31*
Sankova, Galina, photograph by, *50*
Scherrer, Jean-Louis, fashions by, *28-29*
Schumann, Paul, 15; photograph by, *15*
Seattle Times, The, 12; photograph from, *21*
Sedic XF cameras, *158*
Sekonic L-428 meter, *164*
Shinoyama, Kishin, 196; *A Fine Day,* 196, *197-199*
Shore, Henrietta, 66; drawings by, *67*
Shows: William Eggleston, *43,* 56,

57-63; Soviet War Photo-Reportage 1941-1945, 44, *45-55;* Edward Weston, 64, 69, *70-80*
Sigma XQ 39-80mm f/3.5 lens, *163*
Silver dye-bleach process, 148; chemical stages, *150-151;* history, 148-149. *See also* Cibachrome
Siskind, Aaron, 234
Smith, Aileen, 182
Smith, W. Eugene, 168; photograph by, *182*
Society for Photography, German, 180
"Soviet War Photo-Reportage 1941-1945," 44; photographs from, *45-55*
Soligor C-D 35-105 f/3.5 lens, *163*
Sommer, Frederick, 234
Spiratone Aqua Housing, 161
Sports Council (Great Britain), 167
Stieglitz, Alfred, and Walker Evans, 220
Stryker, Roy, 230; obituary, 231
Sun 38-90mm f/3.5 lens, *163*
Sunday Oregonian, The, photograph from, *18-19*
Szarkowski, John, 68; quoted on Edward Weston, 68-69

Talbot, William Henry Fox, 233
Tanuma, Takeyoshi, photograph by, *172*
Tarasevich, Vsevolod, photograph by, *179*
Tomatsu, Shomei, photograph by, *170*
Topeka Capital-Journal, 12
Topeka Daily Capital, The, photograph from, *17*
Trakhman, Mikhail, 48; photograph by, *48*
Tsukahara, Takuya, photograph by, *174*
Turbeville, Deborah, 24, 25, *27;* photographs by, *27-31;* quoted, 26, 27

Ueda, Shoji, photograph by, *169*
Uelsmann, Jerry N., 200; *Silver Meditations,* 200, *201-207*

Underwater equipment: cameras, *161;* housings, 161
Ungaro, fashions by, *28-29*
Unicolor-Mitchell Focusing-Aide, *164*
Union of Soviet Journalists, 179
University of Missouri School of Journalism, 175
Uzian, Alexandr, 47; photographs by, *47*

Vachon, John, obituary, 230-231; photograph by, 230
Van Dyke, Willard, 68
Velazquez, 146, 147
Vienna, photo wall, *232*
Vivitar: Model 283 electronic flash, *162;* Series 1 90mm f/2.5 lens, *163;* Series 1 35-38mm f/2.8 lens, 163
Vogue: fashion photography in, 24, 25; and Herbert List, 231

Washington Post, The, photographs from, *17, 22*
Waterman, Dave, photograph by, 167
Weston, Edward, 64, *65,* 200, 231; in Carmel, 66-68; early life, 64; in Glendale, 64-65; in Mexico, 65-66; photographs by, 68, *70-80;* near Point Lobos, 68-69; quoted, 65, 67; retrospective, 64, 68, 69; techniques, 70
Wheeler, Linda, photograph by, 22
White, Minor, 200
Wilson, Charis, 68
Wilson, Harold, *126*
World War II, Soviet photographs of, *45-55*

Yamamura, Kunio, photograph by, *173*
Yanagisawa, Shin, *83,* 106; photographs by, *107-111*
Yashica: Contax RTS, 159; corporate changes, 233

Zeiss, Karl, Contax RTS, 159
Zelma, Georgi, photograph by, *51*

Printed in U.S.A.